C000112641

Advance Prai
Workout for th

"This clear and informative book offers its readers an invaluable key to mental and spiritual fulfillment."

> —Dr. Richard Lawrence, international best-selling author of *The Meditation Plan, Realize Your Inner Potential,* and *Journey into Supermind*

"This innovative book offers a simple step-by-step exercise program for inner fitness. If we work on our spiritual life we can be successful in everything we do."

> —Dr. John Holder, Chairman, Chelsea Financial Services, Ltd., London, England

"At last a truly practical book about how to survive these stress-filled times. A book full of inspired spiritual practices that will enhance one's sense of inner well-being as well as giving greater outer confidence and poise. A step-by-step guide through an easily understood program of personal spiritual growth and development that will prove of inestimable value to the reader/practitioner."

> —Dave Davies, international rock star, Rock and Roll Hall of Fame; lead guitarist, writer and founder member of The Kinks; author of *Kink*

"I was totally impressed with Chrissie Blaze' book. *Workout for the Soul* is an elegant concept, and well executed. I think it's an original approach that is easily communicated on talk shows, and the details of her program seem to bear up well too. In fact, this is one book I'd love to have bound on my bookshelf so I could reread it and maybe follow the program."

> —Dr. Marcia Yudkin

"*Workout for the Soul* is as essential to our inner journey as Rand McNally is to our next road trip. Cutting across a literary landscape cluttered with spiritual self–help books, Chrissie Blaze delivers where so many have failed. Fortunately for us, she has successfully compressed over 20 years of personal experience in advanced metaphysical practices into a clearly written action plan.

Her program delivers results from day one, and keeps getting better! *Workout for the Soul* is my new companion for life. It will serve as my personal tour guide to higher states of consciousness."

—Ron Davis, President, American Institute of Education, Long Beach, California

"Workout for the Soul is like a breath of fresh air to the new age movement. It can help both new and experienced seekers expand their spirituality in our current materialistic world. I recommend it to everyone on the path in these difficult days—after all, everyone can use a workout for their soul."

—Brian C. Keneipp, Author, *Operation Earth Light: A Glimpse into the World of the Ascended Masters*

Workout for the Soul
Eight Steps to Inner Fitness

Chrissie Blaze

Published by

Aslan
PUBLISHING

Fairfield, CT 06432

Aslan Publishing
2490 Black Rock Turnpike, #342
Fairfield, CT 06432
Please contact the publisher for a free catalog.
Phone: **203/372-0300**
Fax: **203/374-4766**
www.aslanpublishing.com

IMPORTANT NOTE TO READERS:

The opinions and beliefs expressed in this book are those of the author, and do not necessarily represent the views of the publisher. The suggestions contained in this book for personal/spiritual growth are not meant to substitute for the advice of a licensed professional such as a psychologist or psychiatrist. The publishers and author expressly disclaim any liability for injuries resulting from use by readers of the methods contained herein.

Library of Congress Cataloging-in-Publication Data

Blaze, Chrissie.
    Workout for the soul: eight steps to inner fitness / Chrissie Blaze.
        p. cm.
    Includes bibliographical references.
    ISBN 0-944031-90-0
    1. Spiritual exercises. I. Title.

BV4509.2 .B53 2001
291.4'46--dc21

                                        2001022962

Edited by Marcia Yudkin
Book design and illustrations by Dianne Schilling
Cover design by Miggs Burroughs
Printing by Baker Johnson, Inc.
Printed in the USA

Aslan Publishing — Our Mission

Aslan Publishing offers readers a window to the soul via well-crafted and practical self-help books, inspirational books and modern day parables. Our mission is to publish books that uplift the mind, body and spirit.

Living one's spirituality in business, relationships and personal growth is the underlying purpose of our publishing company, and the meaning behind our name, Aslan Publishing. We see the word "Aslan" as a metaphor for living spiritually in the physical world.

Aslan means "lion" in several Middle Eastern languages. The most famous "Aslan" is a lion in *The Chronicles of Narnia* by C.S. Lewis. In these stories, Aslan is the Messiah, the One who appears at critical points in the story in order to point human beings in the right direction. Aslan doesn't preach, he acts. His actions are an inherent expression of who he is.

We hope to point individuals toward joyful, satisfying and healthy relationships with oneself and with others. Our goal is to make a real difference in the everyday lives of our readers.

—*Barbara & Harold Levine, Publishers*

Aslan
PUBLISHING

*This book is dedicated in thankfulness
to my beloved Master, Dr. George King.
His unique global mission of peace and enlightenment
elevated the lives of all of us on Earth.
I know that one day he will be known and revered
by all spiritual aspirants and caring humans
as one who helped to lead us from darkness into Light.
His amazing life and spiritual mission were beyond compare.
His gifts of wisdom, truth and compassion
light years ahead of us mere mortals.
He was the inspiration behind this book
and will remain my inspiration for many, many lives to come.*

Foreword

When I first met Chrissie Blaze some eighteen years ago, she was a loyal and prominent member of the metaphysical organization, The Aetherius Society. I was immediately taken by her sparkling personality, her openmindedness and engaging demeanor. I found her cheerful and positive approach to metaphysics both refreshing and stimulating.

Armed with a profound knowledge of astrology and other meta-sciences, Chrissie Blaze reveals herself to be a modern day spiritual teacher and mystic of high order and influence. Chrissie is an experienced spiritual healer and speaker on spiritual and metaphysical matters and has lectured extensively on these subjects for many years with great eloquence, clarity and effectiveness. Her inner knowledge and spiritual radiance pervade her whole being and she is an inspiration to all her know her.

As an ordained minister and Priest-Elect in The Aetherius Churches, Chrissie's depth of knowledge in yoga, psychic phenomena, healing and divination is indeed impressive and I rejoice in the publication of her book, which I am sure will uplift and inform the reader, as it has me. This is a work that I feel confident will form an integral part of any spiritual library, now or in the future.

In this work, Chrissie presents a concise, practical, insightful and in-depth study of metaphysics — subject matter that is of paramount importance as we enter the new millennium. In an endearing and no-nonsense style, Chrissie provides you with techniques and a methodology that really work, that will help you to feel better, and enable you to help others more effectively.

This book is of inestimable value to the student on the spiritual path, as well as those of us who may still be searching and learning. Good teachers are able to demonstrate their knowledge through interesting and lucid illustrations based on personal experience, and Chrissie does that delightfully, throughout.

In modern society the pressures of daily life often hinder and distract the individual from his or her "true" quest, which I believe to be the awakening of spiritual truth and the realization of personal divinity and the oneness of all things. The search within is the most important journey any one of us can undertake.

As a musician who has been on hundreds of tours and performed in front of many thousands of people worldwide, I have had my fair share of problems and extreme stress. Over the years I have developed my own personal spiritual practices, drawn from many sources. However, I believe that the spiritual practices and wisdom contained in this book will make a profound difference to the sincere aspirant. They will bring inner peace, greater inspiration and wisdom, and the ability to heal and help oneself and others.

I have spent years studying the teachings of many great spiritual teachers and was privileged to know one modern day master, the late Dr. George King, from whom many of the techniques in this book are drawn. The beauty of this book is that Chrissie takes us step-by-step through an inner workout that can be practiced quickly and surely by anyone and everyone to bring tremendous benefits in just a few minutes a day.

The purpose of human life is the cultivation of spiritual knowledge, and you can do no better than to start right here. I know that you will be inspired and enlightened by Chrissie's wonderful and illuminating work. This is a book that will help the true seeker — a book will shed much light upon the path, as it unfolds before you — a practical book full of effective techniques that can help you to make a positive difference in our suffering world.

> —Dave Davies, international rock star, Rock and Roll Hall of Fame; lead guitarist, writer and founding member of The Kinks; author of the autobiography, *Kink.*

Acknowledgements

My thanks go to all my wonderful family for always being there for me. I thank my husband, Gary for his wisdom and love and my parents, Phyllis and Tom Shafe, for their loving support. I especially thank my mother for her grammatical advice.

I am fortunate to have some amazing friends around the world and take this opportunity to thank them all. Of these, I give special thanks to Dr. John Holder for his belief in this project and for his support of it; Dr. Richard Lawrence, Lesley Young, Brian Keneipp, Alyson Lawrence, Raymond Nielsen, Alan Moseley, Dave Davies, Susan Holder, Suzanne McBride and Ron Davis for their encouragement and advice.

I give special thanks to my agent and friend, Sandy Choron, and Barbara and Hal Levine for being excited enough by the concept of this book to make it a reality. I also thank Marcia Yudkin, Dianne Schilling and Miggs Burroughs for their creative and perceptive work.

I am also grateful to the International Directors of The Aetherius Society for giving me permission to quote freely from the wonderful aphorisms and spiritual practices of my incredible Master, Dr. George King.

Contents

Contents

List of Diagrams

List of Exercises

Preface

There is an intelligent Force in the universe unfolding a master plan for the evolution of creation. We are all part of this plan. If we look at the stars, planets, animals and plants, we observe an orderly universe. Everything has a place and a reason for being. Mankind's problems exist because we have not yet found our place in creation. We have not yet, as a whole, realized that we, too, are affected by its inevitable laws, just as surely as the tides of the ocean or the rising of the sun each day. Our selfish desires lead us further down the path of separation. We are isolated by our egos and our demands to do what we want whenever we want — just because we want it!

It is only when we start to listen to the guidance of the still, small voice within — the voice of our soul — that we sense the harmony and majesty of the great laws that can set us free. We sense the oneness of life. We realize that, just as the Sun constantly radiates its life-giving powers throughout the solar system, so too must we radiate our love outwards for the benefit of all. Just as the great Earth beneath us gives freely of her fruits, so too must we support and nurture her, as well as those around us.

Once we sense and realize these things, our desires start to become spiritual ones. Our greatest desires are no longer purely materialistic, for we now recognize the transient nature of materialism. Now we desire greater intuition, more compassion, courage and inner growth. Our heroes are no longer film stars or politicians — but the inspired artists, doctors, musicians, writers and scientists who have moved civilization forward; or the ordinary person, who displays extraordinary kindness or strength of character. Now we are moved by the plight of others and can feel the pain of people we have never met.

It is when these things begin to happen to us that we are on our way to finding a lasting solution to our problems. It is when we yearn to give, rather than take; it is when our feelings of love are stronger than our feelings of hatred; when our desire to be kind is far more compelling than our wish to hurt others, that we begin to find true freedom.

Then we learn that we are not victims of chance but are responsible for our every thought and action. There is now a greater urge to find our destiny, and we feel more than ever that we must listen to and follow the guidance of our conscience — an aspect of our higher self, or soul. The best way to obtain this inner guidance is to go deeper within ourselves, and the best way to do this is to perform spiritual practices.

A friend of mine was recently grieving over the loss of a beloved pet. Her spiritual life was extremely important to her but at this time of grief she stopped all her spiritual practices and fell apart. Although at times like this our practices may be the last thing we feel like doing, the secret is to do them anyway. They are especially helpful during difficult emotional times, times of ill health, or periods of mental stress. We do not stop cleaning our teeth at these times, nor should we stop our spiritual practices. Regard them in this way — as an essential part of your daily routine. Treat them with far more respect than your teeth cleaning and they will eventually become an integral part of your life. Once we realize that our spiritual self is the most enduring and important part of us, we begin to realize how precious our spiritual practices are. The more respect and love we give to them, the more we benefit.

A problem we all face is a lack of time. We all seem to be short of this essential commodity. There will be times when you just cannot squeeze another fifteen minutes out of your day to do this workout. Even so, you should try and do something. It may be a silent prayer of thankfulness, healing energy sent to a sick person, or the holy Practice of the Violet Flame. It will only take a few seconds of your time, but it will make a difference. Remember that every step you take on your spiritual path — no matter how small it may appear to be — is a lasting step that can never be lost. With every practice you are laying a sure foundation stone that will guarantee a better future.

This book gives you the steps that lead to a balanced and potent Workout for the Soul. The workout is a powerful set of spiritual practices designed to benefit you as well as others. It can be practiced by anyone — whatever their religious beliefs — and incorporates mystic practices from the East, as well as the West. It can be performed in only fifteen minutes per day, but can of course be extended to whatever length you wish. However, the aim is that you make this a regular part of your day so that your soul will begin to find fuller expression in your life, to bring greater fulfillment and joy, as well as physical, mental and spiritual balance.

The benefits from the system of spiritual practices in this book — your 15-minute Workout for the Soul — can be many and lasting, but they will depend upon your efforts. The more concentration, feeling, direction and love you put into this, the more you will benefit. In this way, the dynamic system I have outlined is no different from any other kind of physical or mental workout.

Through your improved breathing, concentration and visualization you may gain better health, greater dynamism and clarity of mind. Through your prayers and healing, you may feel fulfillment and inner joy as well as more personal magnetism and energy. You can begin to open your higher psychic centers — the gateways to your soul — and build a lasting bridge to the wonders of your superconscious mind. The results will be greater intuition, and inspiration that can imbue your entire life.

Some people may experience a deep inner satisfaction that they are growing spiritually and are able to make a difference to our world and to our future. Many experience feelings of inner peace and of being more in control of their lives. If you perform this workout regularly, you will begin to find answers to questions that may have previously remained unanswered. Through this

Workout for the Soul you can find your own destiny and place in life. The practices will teach you how to recognize spiritual opportunities and how to be more open to change and creative self-expression.

Above all, the greatest benefit is that you will begin to express more fully the spiritual potential within. *Workout for the Soul* offers a type of spiritual protection and, though things may not always be easy, you will have greater strength to learn from your experiences and move on. These practices will give you the groundwork from which you can overcome the weaknesses that now hold you back.

Workout for the Soul is different from most other self-development books. While this book can bring you all the above benefits, that is not its main focus. Above all, it was written to teach you how to help others in a more powerful way — for this is the key to spiritual development.

For once, let's take the emphasis away from us and get on with the most important job of all — becoming a light in our dark world. However dim your light may be at the moment, if you take this book to heart and practice the Workout for the Soul, you can fan your inner light into a brilliant flame, to sustain you, your family, your friends — and even strangers.

The more you do this, the more you can illuminate the world, and it is then that the darkness can no longer exist. This is the way forward. The only price you must pay initially is fifteen minutes of your time each day. The secret is not to think about it, or to dream of it, but just to do it. This is the key and the only key. The more you do it, the better you will be. It is that simple.

You owe it to yourself because you are worth the effort it takes to express the riches within your soul. You owe it to the world because you are an integral part of the global family and of creation itself. As such, everything you think and everything you do affects your future, the future of your children, your children's children — and everything else in creation.

The real answers to our problems do not lie in politics or academic theory, but in the selfless efforts of every concerned person on earth. Practical spirituality is the global language — and it offers the global solution to our problems, as well as the way to our personal advancement. There are many religions and positive belief systems that abound on Earth at this time — which is good — but they should serve to join us not to divide us. At this crisis point in our history, the important thing is that we join together in selfless, spiritual ways to help our world.

Just as many good men and women are working hard in practical, physical ways to help feed the hungry, heal the sick and preserve the delicate ecological balance, so too should we work in spiritual ways to harmonize and balance the whole. When we send healing power to a sick person, the energy works to bring balance to his or her physical body. So it is with our world. All of our prayers and healing work will bring balance to the surface of our world so that growth, health and abundance must eventually result.

Workout for the Soul is a powerful way to help in this global mission for peace and enlightenment — which is the responsibility and destiny of us all.

Introduction
The Eternal Quest

By our thoughts and actions of today, we carve tomorrow.
—George King

A saint is a sinner who never gives up.
—Paramahansa Yogananda

Life is a series of journeys. Each journey starts with an initial step that requires our courage and faith. Completing the journey takes determination and will. Whether it is a physical journey, a mental journey or a spiritual one, the ingredients for success are the same. The spiritual journey is the most difficult one of all and the most rewarding. Why? Because we are so used to scratching the surface of life that going deep within ourselves requires greater effort and commitment. It is the most rewarding because with spiritual growth we learn that the journey is in fact the goal.

I have devised this book as a simple system to help you begin this spiritual journey to inner fitness, self-mastery and soul development. The system can be learned easily and performed in only fifteen minutes, but its benefits are numerous and the results will last forever.

Every person in history who has attained self-mastery has started his or her inner journey at the same place as you or me. My spiritual teacher, Dr. George King, was an extremely unusual and advanced man. At the age of twelve he went into the woods one day and was inspired to send healing to his sick mother; shortly afterwards she was completely cured of a life-threatening illness. Such occurrences, commonly regarded as miracles, became a part of his everyday life. He went on to discover that healing could be done on not only an individual level, but on a global scale. This became part of his life's mission, which was an exceptional one.

Just as you are about to do now, Dr. King sat down one day and started a series of spiritual practices. After years of intense and diligent practice for many hours each day, he eventually attained enlightenment and became a master of many forms of yoga. He attained ultimate self-mastery, the elevated state of "union with God" known in the East as *samadhi*. He no longer just believed things were true; now he was a "knower." He could understand the real mysteries of creation and had discovered the world of lasting inner bliss. However, his personal advancement led him to realize that he must leave this rich, inner world in order to give his power, strength, courage and inspiration in the service of mankind.

You may have begun your journey to go deeper, to understand more and express the divinity within. You may have already heard the voice of your higher self. You may have been through experiences that, in retrospect, have served to move you from an egocentric groove to a more God-centered place. It is usually at this point that we become aware that our true mission in life is not just about earning a decent living and having lots of nice things. Although the full blossoming of divine powers may still be far from our minds, we begin to make more conscious choices towards what is right, and feel more aware that we are all just a small part of something huge. We then start to feel frustrated at our ignorance, whereas previously we were satisfied. At this point we yearn to know our true destiny and to fathom the mysteries of our inner self.

The biography of Viktor Frankl is very inspiring, for it was through his own personal suffering that he learned the vital importance of the soul and inner fitness. A respected psychiatrist in Vienna, he was captured by the Nazis in World War II and thrown into a concentration camp, where he endured terrible years of imprisonment. The terrible hardship and limitation he endured there forced him to go within, so that he discovered many things about the human condition.

Frankl's discoveries — which were fundamental to the ancient mystics — were that every man and woman has an innate human impulse to understand the purpose of life. He found through his further studies that if this impulse is thwarted, the result is sickness. He found that not only outer conditions make us sick, but also inner struggles and frustrations. The latter represent a real part of our desire to discover just what we are born to do. The Workout for the Soul will, if practiced, help us in our inner journey and enable us to find our place in life, so that our own frustrations can be healed at a deep level.

Some of you may have already been practicing concentration, contemplation or some form of meditation; some of you may be practicing pranayama or breathing exercises; others may be students of yoga. Some of you, I am sure, may be taking this journey for the first time. It does not matter, because you will all start at the same point in this program. If you have done these types of exercises before you will probably achieve results quicker, but if you are new to spiritual development the results will come just the same.

What are my qualifications to write such a book? My expertise lies in the world of metaphysics, yoga and the spiritual sciences. I began my studies into the psychic and spiritual realms in the 1960s, at the age of 14. My own urge towards personal growth in these areas led me to the fortunate position of meeting my spiritual teacher, Dr. King, whom I recognized as an extremely unusual and advanced man and master. The more I studied his teachings and learned from him, the more I appreciated the extent of his wisdom and advanced metaphysical knowledge. I eventually became a close student and disciple of his for twenty-three years until his demise.

Dr. King expressed the highest aspirations with every breath he took. His life was a mission for world peace and enlightenment;

all of his energy, his genius and his scientific and spiritual knowledge went towards this end. He passed on in 1997 and left behind him a spiritual legacy that will not be fully understood for decades. One of the things he taught was that practicality is the key in this new millennium — not theories, hopes or wishes, but practical action. Several of his remarkable practices and initiations are distilled into this book, in the hope that they may leave you with a desire to know more of his work and teachings.

When I first started my own inner journey, I spent years finding the techniques that suited me. I have spent hours visualizing different objects, forms and colors in psychic development groups. I have practiced and taught the art of psychometry — divination through touching objects. I have studied and practiced hands-on healing for twenty years and taught it for fifteen years. I have performed breathing exercises in different environments, and have felt the elevating effects of the great Universal Life Forces flowing through me. These Universal Life Forces radiate constantly from the Sun and permeate all life. They are known by different names in different cultures, including *prana* and *chi*.

I have made an intense study and practice of prayer, under the skilled direction of my master, and am now highly experienced in a powerful method of radiating spiritual energy, which he termed "dynamic prayer." I have not only prayed for the plight of mankind, as I am sure you have done many times, but have learned that prayer is one of the greatest of the spiritual sciences that can be used to heal and perform miracles.

For over twenty-five years, I have studied and practiced the science of mantra, a sacred ritual of the repetition of sounds in Sanskrit. By doing this, we can change ourselves as well as our environment for the better. I have had many interesting psychic experiences, as a result of these years of spiritual practices, and I have developed my intuition to a fairly high level so that it is a reliable, trustworthy friend.

One thing I realized is that it is more important to have a system of practices that you can perform at least three times every week than to spend hours one day and then do nothing for several months. It is repetition, practice and more practice that bring results. That is why I have put together these steps. They can be accomplished simply, and the entire Workout for the Soul will take only fifteen minutes. If I set up a complex program that would take you over an hour, most of you would probably do it a few times and then stop. Consistency really is the key to success in spiritual matters, just as it is in every other area of our lives. I believe that this workout will not only be effective in helping you to gain some degree of enlightenment, but will also generate within you a deeper desire to help others and the world as a whole.

Our world needs help. Unfortunately, there has been much conflict and war in our world in the name of religion. The result is that many people are seeking a new understanding, a universal religion — spirituality without dogma or hypocrisy. Over the years, we have seen a deep desire in people of different backgrounds and religious beliefs to manifest their divine potential and to work together with other good-hearted people in the service of mankind. The word "service" is often misunderstood and is certainly not a popular concept. It is, however, far more beneficial than is work alone. When we work we produce things, but when we serve, we become something; as such service is a vitally important part of our soul growth and an essential part of this workout.

Edgar Cayce, who helped millions of people with his famous life-readings, summed up service in another way when he said: "Know that the purpose for which each soul enters a material experience is that it may be a light unto others." Only when we realize this do we begin to find the deeper inner fulfillment of our soul's purpose.

In Greek mythology, Theseus, a great king and hero of Athens, went down to the netherworld, where the lord of the netherworld offered him a chair. Theseus didn't realize that it was the chair of forgetfulness and he sat down and instantly forgot everything. He forgot who he was, where he came from, and why he had come down to the netherworld in the first place. He just sat there until Hercules came and got him out. This story is an allegory about human beings. We have forgotten what we are and why we are here. We are not physical beings striving to be spiritual; we are spiritual beings in physical bodies. We are all sparks of God, and we only have to remember it, realize it and then learn how to re-awaken our divine nature.

Material life constantly encourages us to be superficial. We are judged not so much by our character, our integrity, our honesty and our spirituality, but by how well we fit into the standards laid down by those who wish us to conform. Whether you are a parent or the president of a country, it is far easier to deal with a family or a nation of pleasant, apathetic sheep, than a group of vital, vibrant, independent, courageous, self-motivated, spiritually-minded individuals. It is, however, the latter group who change our world for the better; the former just maintain the status quo, no matter how corrupt it may become.

This book is not for the sheep among us, who blindly follow the latest trend or fashion. It is for the rare person who is able to think for him or herself, who realizes that the purpose of life is not just to have possessions and material aspirations but is something far nobler, deeper and richer than that.

This book is for people who are probably far from perfect, but who have a spirit of enquiry and adventure. Such individuals are aware of the deeper part of their nature and have questions that most people cannot begin to answer. They are dissatisfied with the 9 to 5 daily routine and are prepared to spend precious time in a quest that does not necessarily bring more money or friends. They have the romanticism to believe in the Holy Grail and the realism to know that it resides within. They have the idealism associated with the spiritual quest and the practicality to know that it takes work to bring that part alive. They are moved by the suffering in the world, and frustrated not to be able to help more. Such individuals are prepared to strive to become more each day and, when a mistake is made, brush themselves off and start over.

In other words, I wrote this book for the brave, honest soul who, although not yet a spiritual adept, a yogi, or an enlightened master or guru, has within faith and belief in the limitless power of divinity. I wrote this book for the person who knows that he or she can really make a difference.

Workout for the Soul is not about self-knowledge, although that is a part of it. It is not about self-realization, although that is essential. It is about expressing your divinity, realizing that we are all One, and working towards the enlightenment of all mankind. By having the very highest motive, you will obtain the best results and your own progress will be that much more successful.

Most of us reading this book are in the fortunate position of having a roof over our heads at night. We have two or three meals each day, probably a job, a car and regular vacations. Many of us have families and friends whom we love, and we take regular trips out to dinner, a movie and the local shopping mall. Many of us have a college education and are in reasonable health. We may even make fairly regular trips to the local gym. We never seem to have enough money, but somehow we always get by. Our hearts go out to those less fortunate and to people around the world who are suffering.

Most of us reading this book are moved by poverty and contribute regularly to a charity of our choice. We are pretty good on the whole and are ready to lend a helping hand. We are among the most fortunate people on Earth and many of us, realizing that there is more, search for the next step. This step is towards personal growth, self-development, and advancement. We have read books that tell us we are only using a small portion of our potential and want to use more.

Many of us are inspired by people who have done this — athletes, scientists, artists, adventurers of every kind — because deep down we know that we have the willpower and the urge to push ourselves further, just as they have done. Most thinking people realize that we are not born in order to live in contentment and procrastination, but we are here to contribute to the advancement of mankind in some way, to take control of our lives and to push the limits that bind us that much further. We instinctively know that all advancement on this planet stems from this urge, this desire, this will to move mountains. We are the "salt of the Earth," the ordinary person, the fortunate person who doesn't have to struggle just to survive. We are truly blessed.

This book is the result of years of study and more important, practice. Although time spent lifting weights at the gym, or performing some other kind of exercise, is important to keep our physical bodies in shape, the Workout for the Soul is more important. Through doing this we can improve our health, our mental powers and above all, begin to consciously express our soul qualities. We then start to advance along the path of spiritual evolution — the ultimate quest of us all.

Many people will sacrifice a good deal of their spare time to get fit. They will struggle, sweat and suffer for many hours each week to get in shape, which is a good thing. I wondered why these people, who are obviously interested in self-improvement, would not put the same amount of effort, energy and sweat into improving their inner fitness. I came to the following conclusions:

1. There is confusion about exactly what the soul is and about its importance.
2. Even when the nature of the soul is understood, that the soul can be "exercised" is not generally realized.
3. There are few simple workouts for the soul available that we can slot into our busy lives.

Let's now look at these factors one by one.

1. The Relationship Between the Soul and the Spirit

The following passage from Dr. George King's *Contact Your Higher Self Through Yoga* is a brilliant description of the relationship between our soul and spirit.

> *Imagine a radiant, angelic being, clothed in the dazzling white robes of purity, riding in a chariot pulled by two strong, fleet horses through the golden gates of a magnificent temple. This angelic being, beautiful beyond all description, is symbolic of the spark of divinity within you — the spirit. The will he exerts, through his hands, over his horse, represents the part played by your soul. His guiding hands, your mind and the powerful horses, prana. While the chariot symbolizes your physical body and the temple, his destination, represents God, which the eventual destination of every soul. This is a*

poor illustration but it is hoped that it may, at least, serve to ex-
plain the part played by the spirit and by prana, which is the vital
energy that is used by the divine spirit through the will in the
journey through evolution.

Deep within us, we have a part of God Itself — the spirit.
This aspect, although often cloaked by thick layers in many of us,
binds us together in our journey back to our source.

We stand on the shores of a vast universe that continues to
amaze and inspire us with awe and wonder every time a new
discovery is made. Despite recent developments in rockets, computers, and other marvels of science, we are painfully ignorant of
the world in which we live. We are even more ignorant of our
inner universe, which for some reason many of us have forgotten
about and ignore, despite an ever more urgent need to uncover
the truth of our existence. If we take the time to be silent and
reflect, if we are really honest, somewhere deep within us we know
that something is missing.

Our everyday life has become increasingly competitive, full of
anxiety, disease, stress and the pursuit of materialism. Most of us
are on a seemingly endless treadmill with little relief in sight. Because of this we often develop an inner emptiness, sense of futility
and restlessness. Why? Because by being caught up in the many
traps of material life, we are in effect putting our hands over our
eyes — the mirrors of our souls — and are then left groping in the
dark.

What really is the use of spending all our time and energy on
our worldly dreams? Even if we were to become a great singer, we
would eventually lose our voice; every great athlete eventually has
his or her day. The businessman who amasses a fortune will have
to leave it behind him when he dies. It is only logical, therefore, to
spend at least some time and energy in our lives on increasing our
spiritual wealth, for this never goes to waste. Our spiritual wealth,
which we amass through our good thoughts and actions, will grow
and accumulate in our "spiritual bank account." This spiritual bank
account will pay us dividends forever. Even when we are reborn,

we will be able to reclaim this wealth that will always work for our benefit, for good deeds are never wasted.

When we realize and find God in our lives and when we start to act upon our highest inspirations, our lives will take on a whole new meaning and purpose. Suddenly all the problems in our material lives will seem more easily managed and less important, and some may vanish altogether.

2. Can the Soul Be "Exercised?"

The next problem many of us have about developing our inner fitness is that we believe God is within anyway, so why do we have to work at it? If we take one moment's thought, it is obvious that we must do so. Every mystic, every saint, every great person had to struggle and make tremendous sacrifices and efforts on their spiritual path. Advancement only comes to us, in any aspect of our life, if we put our concentration, effort and will behind it.

A popular aphorism is that "Inspiration is 99 percent perspiration." Anyone who has attained some degree of inspiration, whether through the arts or the sciences, knows the bliss of that feeling of breakthrough. Suddenly, everything flows through you in a way that seems to come from outside of yourself. When you read what you have written, or look at what you have painted or created, even you — the inspired one — are amazed at the results.

For most of us, these moments are fleeting, but when they come they are worth all the previous effort. The shout of "Eureka!" usually includes relief from all the mental pressure and hard work we have exerted up to that point. It is like the Sun shining through the clouds; it is breakthrough. It is our limited conscious mind finally making that connection inwards to our super-conscious mind. We all have a super-conscious mind from which we can gain inspiration and high intuition, but these jewels are only revealed to us through hard work and effort in the right way.

You may know people who were born geniuses, who are truly inspired, seemingly without effort. However, somewhere down the line, in one life or another, they must have worked hard to reach this point. The inspiration, vision and hard work of the few are the building blocks of the evolution of our race; they enable us all to progress on our journey of scientific, technological and artistic discovery. Their giant steps on behalf of humanity help us all in the most important journey of all to grow, to think more clearly and deeply and to awaken.

Not only should we work at our self-mastery and growth, we also must do so with regularity. We cannot just make one great attempt and expect our goal to be reached. It is like anything else. Let us take a fruit tree as an example. After the seed has been planted it first sprouts and then eventually grows into a tree. Before it can produce fruit, a specific amount of time must pass. Further, the tree must be exposed to a certain amount of light and heat and consume a certain amount of nutrients and water. If it does not get these elements in appropriate amounts and at the appropriate time, the tree's growth will be stunted; it may even die before reaching maturity. If it is deprived of the proper amount of light for months and is suddenly bombarded by intense light for days at a time, just imagine what will happen to that poor tree. Our soul, like the tree, must be nurtured and encouraged in the same way through steady, regular practice.

3. A Balanced Workout for the Soul

In order to advance, we must give our souls a workout, just as we do the physical and mental aspects of ourselves that we wish to improve, and we then need an effective way to do it. There are many books on yoga and the spiritual sciences that teach the path to enlightenment. Yoga means "union with God," and there are many different paths of yoga we can take in order to find the God within. These range from the popular Hatha Yoga, which consists of physical postures, to the many other forms of yoga, little known in the West, such as Gnani Yoga, Raja Yoga, Karma Yoga, Mantra Yoga, Mudra Yoga, Kundalini Yoga and others.

As mentioned, I have practiced and taught aspects of several of these forms of yoga, as well as many of the spiritual sciences. However, I have drawn upon the teachings of my Master and those from ancient wisdom, and designed this Workout for the Soul so that anyone can use it, whether or not they have any knowledge of yoga and metaphysics. To really advance in spiritual ways takes hours of time, effort, and energy each day, just as to really become a world-class athlete you must be completely dedicated to your success. However, this book serves as a starting point. It consists of simple, progressive steps that lead to a simple workout that can be performed in just fifteen minutes a day.

Why should you bother to do this at all? The benefits include greater dynamism and personal magnetism, better concentration, more accessible intuitive powers, greater self-confidence, more understanding of your own unique destiny, better health, inner joy and fulfillment. However, in the quest for inner fitness, the ultimate goal is to become more fully human by first realizing the God potential within and then expressing this for the benefit of all. In the ultimate quest, the journey back to God becomes the goal.

The great mystic and scientist, Albert Einstein, summed it up when he said:

> A human being is part of the whole, called by us 'universe,' a part limited in space and time. He experiences himself, his thoughts and feelings, as something separate from the rest, a kind of optical delusion of consciousness. This delusion is kind of a prison for us restricting us to our personal desires and to affection for a few persons nearest to us. Our task must be to free ourselves from this prison by widening our circle of compassion to embrace all living creatures and the whole of nature in its beauty.

This book, *Fifteen-Minute Workout for the Soul*, will — if used — liberate us from the prison Einstein described. Many of us have an innate desire to keep our lives as they are, but once we start to glimpse the wonder and beauty that is within us, we will not hesitate to delve even deeper. We will be like the man dying of thirst in the desert who sees an oasis just before him. He does not just stop there and stare; he is filled with hope and joy at the glimpse of this sparkling water, just as our souls will delight when they glimpse the sparkling waters of truth and wonder that reside within us all — the Spark of God.

In the words of the great Yoga Master, Sri Ramakrishna:

When you add zeros successively to the digit one, you get figures whose value increases proportionally; a hundred, a thousand, a million, etc., but without the digit one before them, they are of no value. Similarly God is the "number one" in all the values of life. If you leave Him out of the picture in life's pursuits, those pursuits become a string of worthless zeros.

My own Master followed on from this thought when he said:

The proof of the existence of God is not found within books, nor in the words of others, the proof is hidden within ourselves and we must make the effort to manifest this.

The First Steps

These first steps involve character-building, which is essential on any spiritual path. They are steps of faith, hope, bravery, love and perseverance — the keys to success in every spiritual endeavor.

Many people attempt to live at a superficial level, skating across the surface. Unfortunately, the wake-up call usually comes through painful experience. The universe doesn't care about our career status, the make of car we have or whether we live in the right part of town. We are conditioned to think that to be responsible we must have all these things, which continues to stifle our soul. What is our real responsibility? It is to break free of the limitations of convention by thinking our own thoughts, by trusting in our intuition and by applying discrimination and awakening our full potential.

In this journey of courage, the first brave step we must take is to analyze and challenge even our own beliefs and prejudices. If we do so, then at every step of the journey we will find ourselves opening up to forces beyond our comprehension. Again, it will take courage to go deeper, beyond where we have gone before, into the uncharted territories of our inner self and the nature of our soul. *Fifteen-Minute Workout for the Soul* will help us do that.

First we must take that leap of faith before we will do anything different from our normal routine; most of us are resistant to change, even when we know intuitively that the time has come for us to do so. We feel we can no longer hold onto the past, but are afraid to go forward into an unknown future. That is why so many people desperately try to stay where they are, afraid to change and not sure how to do so anyway. However, once we have taken the leap of faith, we will find that although we may not yet be able to fly, we can experience equally magical things. By practicing the Workout for the Soul you are taking a leap of faith.

There are so many distractions in life, so very many things that will try and pull us off our paths. Even if you complete the steps in this book and enjoy them, you will still find it difficult to commit to this workout, even though it takes only a few minutes of your time. However, the more you persist, the more you will build your soul qualities of will and strength, which will help you to continue. Perseverance and practice really are the keys, just as in learning and acquiring any new skill. The rewards with this particular skill — soul awakening — are far greater, and they will last forever and ever. Every day you can build a stronger bridge to the jewels that reside within you.

How to Use This Book

I designed this as a spiritual workbook. I did not intend it to be read once and then discarded. It is designed as a practical course to be read, studied and, above all, practiced. I know most authors wish that for their books, but I believe this one is different from most. In fifteen minutes a day you won't just become a better writer, carpenter or cook; you will become a better person. If you regularly practice these exercises, you will not only change your own life for the better, but you will also help to make a better world.

The first eight chapters of the book consist of eight practical and progressive steps. At the end of each of these is a set of simple exercises. Practice these exercises diligently for one week before you continue with the next step. At the end of the eight steps you will then be ready to practice the fifteen-minute workout that is based upon the previous steps. This is the Workout for the Soul, a simple, balanced and potent program for your advancement. Continue with this workout for at least three days every week. The more you practice, the more benefits and results you will obtain.

I must stress that this book gives an ideal scenario for your Workout for the Soul. If followed precisely, it will bring you greater strength, dynamism, courage, intuition and inspiration. However, there will be times in your life when you do not have ideal conditions and will feel tempted to stop. At these times, do not worry about the conditions; don't let anything get in the way of your spiritual practices.

After one month you may wish to increase the length of the workout, which you can do simply by spending more time on each part. If you are then getting good results and wish to further enhance your workout, follow the steps given in the last chapter, "Enhancing Your Workout."

In *Fifteen-Minute Workout for the Soul,* I can only point you in the right direction and give you the tools to use on your spiritual path to enlightenment. It is up to you to use them. May you be blessed with perseverance on this most important journey. May you, through regular and diligent practice of your Workout for the Soul, be firmly on the road to lasting joy and spiritual enlightenment.

Step One

Preparing the Temple

Come to the edge.
We can't, we are afraid.
Come to the edge.
We can't, we will fall.
Come to the edge —
And they came, and he pushed them
And they flew.
—Guillaume Apollinaire

Strength does not come from physical capacity.
It comes from an indomitable will.
—Mahatma Gandhi

In Step One you will concentrate on creating your own sacred space, as well as enhancing the vibrations of your room and those of your own personal temple, the physical body. All of the guidelines and practices in this step teach ideal conditions that will bring you the very best results, but in time you may wish to adjust and modify some of the preparatory steps to suit your requirements.

I have taught spiritual healing for many years and always show students the ideal way to prepare themselves to give healing. However, I also point out that if a person drops down in front of them, they should not worry about putting on a white coat and performing essential mental exercises before sending that person healing. Ideal settings are important so that we can gain the most benefit from our spiritual work — but they should not be overemphasized. To be an idealist is good but to be a practical idealist is far better!

Creating Your Altar

You must first find a suitable area of your home that you can make your sacred space and dedicate to your Workout for the Soul. This is a space you will reserve exclusively for your spiritual practices, so that in time it becomes imbued with the high vibrations of your meditations, inspirations, prayers and healing work. The more you bring this space alive with spiritual work and uplifting thoughts, the easier it will be for you to connect with your higher self.

We do have a higher self and many of us are aware of this; some are guided by it completely. Our higher self urges us to live in accordance with the great laws of the universe, in the knowledge that only then can true freedom dawn. The majority of us, however, are still battling with our lower selves and the iron grip of our egos. The more you visit your sacred space to contact this true part of your nature, the more the grip of the conscious mind will be lessened. Through your efforts, you will light a spiritual flame in your sacred space that will nourish you and will spread outwards towards the nourishment of the whole world.

Because this area of your home and of your life will become your sanctuary and your spiritual retreat, and the place where you can find great joy, peace and love, it is important that you select it carefully.

Choosing Your Sacred Space

You should choose a space that just feels good to you and where you can, if possible, face east, while performing your daily ritual. The sun – which is constantly radiating the life-giving pranas or universal life forces that are the basis of manifestation in our solar system — rises in the east. The East is always associated with mystical power and spiritual practices, so that facing in this direction will help to enhance your spiritual workout.

Once you have found an area in your home that feels right to you, the next step is to build an altar to focus and enhance your spiritual practices. On your altar you will put photographs and objects that are sacred and significant to you, that uplift and inspire you. This altar does not have to be grand, or even bigger than a few precious objects on a shelf. The important thing is that you love it. In time, your altar and surrounding area will become like your inner sanctuary that is yours alone, which you will want to visit as often as you can. In time, you will find that just looking at your altar will bring you peace and strength.

My own altar is in a quiet room in my apartment. It is quite small and contains nothing but bookshelves holding holy artifacts that I have collected over many years. Although modest, it is now so powerful that I can feel it even when I am outside my home, drawing me into its presence.

If you can afford the space, try and have your own personal altar, rather than share one with another person. My husband has his own altar in another room. His contains articles that are different from mine, ones that are meaningful to him.

Sacred Objects for Your Altar

In order to begin this eight-step program, keep your altar area very simple and gradually build it over time. You may begin with just a picture of your own spiritual master or guru, one of the Indian saints or sages for example, or a beautiful photograph of Mother Earth. The artifacts on my altar include pieces of rock from holy mountains, grains of sand from a sacred beach and blessed water. I also have a candle and incense that I light.

Some of the other objects I have on my altar include a holy cross. The cross has obvious associations with Christianity. This symbol predates Christianity, however, and is a very ancient, mystical symbol that represents the resurrection of the spirit of man through experience back to our Divine Source.

I regard myself as a mystic Christian, but I am also extremely respectful of Buddhism, Judaism, Hinduism and indeed all the other major religions, appreciating the essential truth which lies behind and within all the great religions. I have a beautiful statue of Buddha and several artifacts that are significant to me. I also have a number of powerful wooden shapes, which contain stones from holy mountains, each of which was personally blessed by my Master.

The objects on my altar all have mystical or symbolic meaning to me. Yours will be very personal to you and therefore should be selected by you very carefully. Do not rush the collection process. It may take you years to complete your altar, but you will find that it will grow and unfold as you do. The secret is to hold the thought of your sacred space in your mind whenever you have a moment of quiet. Visualize it being filled with light and power; feel a link with this in your mind's eye and feel the light and power from your altar flowing back to you. If you do this practice you will find that over time wonderful artifacts will be given to you, or you will somehow track them down.

The desire to develop spiritually has great power, and you will start to develop a mystical flow that will bring to you those things that you need for your enlightenment. These objects will be the correct ones for you because of the link you have established with your altar and because of the light and power you have visualized there. This occurs because of the law that what you think and visualize eventually comes into manifestation. Given this law, you must always employ discrimination in your choices, and only use objects that are uplifting and inspirational.

Balancing Through the Five Elements

It is good to have each of the five elements represented during your practices i.e. earth (in the form of a piece of rock or some sand), fire (in the form of a candle or incense), air, ether, and a bowl of water. Ether is the so-called "empty" space between matter and the primary force from which the other elements flow. Using all five elements brings balance and power to the ritual you are about to perform.

Many cultures throughout the world include the five elements in their traditions and rituals. In Tibet, huge structures were built as symbols of the structure of creation. The base of each structure represented earth. On this cube-like base was a sphere that represented water. On top of the sphere was a spiral structure that represented fire and at the very top was a half-moon representing air. In this rested a small sphere representing ether — the fifth element. Ether is the primary force from which the other elements flow.

In the Western tradition the fifth element is not generally mentioned, even though it is important as the source of the other four. The Chinese speak of five elements, though they have a different system comprising fire, air, water, wood and metal. The elements are like unseen builders and ancient traditions say that they must mesh in harmony with each other for health and well-being to exist. Through the elements flow the universal life forces.

The Use of Color

If you have a table or proper altar area, you may wish to cover it with a beautiful piece of cloth. Select vibrant, rich colors that you enjoy and that are mystical and uplifting in quality. Violet, for example, has an extremely high vibration, so shades of violet, purple and magenta are excellent choices.

You can use a green light over or shining onto your altar, which again is extremely beneficial. I give more information on the power and qualities of color in Step Five. The color green is the most harmonious and balancing color and can be shone on anyone safely. Obviously, light has different frequencies and some colors may not be appropriate for one's spiritual practices. I would not use, for example, the stimulating colors such as red. It is safer to use green, which is beneficial to everyone and can greatly assist in your spiritual practices and in lifting the atmosphere in your "temple."

Make sure that you arrange the items on your altar lovingly, carefully and intuitively. The whole effect should be harmonious, balanced and beautiful. My own altar is extremely powerful and I am always aware of its power even before doing any practices. It has a mystical life of its own! Start building your altar until you feel the power build; this will be beneficial to you and those who live with you. It will also offer some protection to your home and family.

Do not wait until you have built the perfect altar before you begin your practices. You will find that your conscious mind is always ready with a million and one excuses to stop you from embarking on your spiritual practices. The most important part is to begin. While the correct preparation will assist you, the key is practice.

Handling Your Sacred Objects

Make it a ritual to clean your altar on a regular basis, as well as keep the room in which your altar is set very clean. Clean your altar very carefully so as not to disturb the high vibrations you have created. Everything has a vibration and everything we touch affects us, just as we affect what we touch. I wear white cotton gloves to move the blessed articles I have so as not to contaminate them with any vibrations I may have inadvertently picked up during the day.

Psychometry is the psychic art of divination through touching objects. The basis for psychometry is that we imprint our vibrations on everything we touch. Depending upon the nature of the material we touch, it can hold these vibrations for hundreds of years. In modern times this fact has been discovered by the quantum physicists, but has been realized for centuries by the sages and mystics: Thought affects and alters matter. By wearing gloves or washing our hands, we protect our sacred objects and show our respect and reverence for them. This is a practice that my Master encouraged when handling sacred objects, as he understood their delicacy and sacredness.

Use of Incense, Lamp or Candle

Throughout the ages, incense has been used to purify, fumigate, heal, uplift and protect our environment, as well as enhance moods. As long ago as 2000 B.C., Chinese, Egyptian and Indian herbalists traded and formulated long-burning incenses for sacramental use. These included frankincense, myrrh, amber and sandalwood. After the invention of essential oil distillation, the science of perfumery expanded throughout Asia, Egypt and Europe, with highly scented flowers like jasmine, rose and lily grown for the perfume trade. By the Italian Renaissance, the addition of essential oils to classical incense offered even more sophisticated results. In East and West alike, incense and aromatic oils have always been an important part of ceremonial practices.

If you are not sure which type of incense to buy, begin with sandalwood, frankincense and myrrh; these are known to be inspirational and uplifting aromas. However, I urge you to experiment until you discover what suits you.

Once you are ready to begin, you should light the incense, which you can purchase in sticks or cones. First ignite the incense, then allow it to smolder, releasing a perfumed smoke. Make sure you invest in good quality incense as it can uplift — or hinder — the vibrations in your sacred space. It is possible to purchase pure botanical essential oils in incense form, and I would highly recommend this. If you are asthmatic, or do not like the smell of incense, then do not use it.

You may prefer to use essential oils in an aroma diffuser to release uplifting aromas into the atmosphere. A diffuser is a small container that is filled with water and heated using a candle. Add 6-10 drops of essential oil to the water in the bowl of the diffuser. Aromatic oils become diffused as the water is heated. As with the incense, ensure that any essential oils you buy are of the purest quality. Look for oils that are calming, balancing, relaxing and uplifting.

There are many wonderful oils you can choose, but again I highly recommend frankincense. This has always been regarded as a sacred oil, with elevating properties as well as being calming for stressful, anxious conditions. It also has the effect of slowing and deepening the breath, which is essential for your spiritual practices. It is helpful and conducive for contemplative and meditative states.

Another good oil to use is sandalwood. This has soothing and balancing properties and has been historically linked with inner awareness and cleansing of the spirit. A personal favorite of mine is lavender. Entire books have been written on the therapeutic effects of lavender. Lavender is known to calm, relax and balance, as well as to purify the atmosphere.

If you have a lamp, or candle, light this also, to assist in building power and creating a pleasant atmosphere before you begin the next step.

Allowing the Vibrations of Your Room to Settle

Once you have created the atmosphere you desire, then you should leave the room for a few minutes to allow the vibrations to settle. Then, when you are ready to begin your spiritual practices, return to the room and attune yourself to the wonderful atmosphere you have created.

Preparing the Temple of Your Soul

There is a trend now to lavish constant attention on our physical bodies. Many people spend hours of their time, hours of other people's time and thousands of dollars on pampering their physical bodies. They clothe themselves with the latest fashions. They work out in the gym, stretch their body, strengthen it and perfect it. They take it to the doctor's; they have it kneaded, pummeled, injected, fortified, purified, cleansed. All this is good, if you have the time and the money to do it, but it is not necessary for your Workout for the Soul. Like the gymnast or the body-builder, you should recognize the importance of your physical body, but not as an end in itself.

Our physical bodies are extremely important as the temples of the soul, the vehicles in which we live and gain experience. We should respect this brilliant, complex "machine" — our physical body — through correct breathing, diet and exercise. If you regard your body in this way, you will feel a certain reverence and love towards your body that will definitely help you in Step One.

Before you begin your spiritual practices, you should shower or take a relaxing bath, if you have the time to do so. Obviously it is very beneficial and relaxing to draw a warm bath sprinkled with aromatic oils. Not only will you clean your physical body but you will also be in a relaxed physical and mental state as preparation for the next steps. There is definitely truth in the aphorism, "Cleanliness is next to Godliness."

The cleaner your skin, the more sensitive it becomes. When you have a bandage on your finger and remove it after a few days, you will see how clean the skin is and how sensitive it feels. These spiritual practices will help you to raise your own vibrations, and this cleansing ritual is an initial step in the process. If you have the time, you should make this an enjoyable, relaxing ritual.

Wearing a Robe or Special Attire

It is not by chance that ordained clergy and priests wear robes for conducting services and performing various rituals and sacraments. One reason for this is that the robes, because of their design, tend to hold the high vibrations radiated during the services. In time, the cloth itself will become imbued with spiritual energies and so enhance the prayers and spiritual outpouring of the wearer. After your shower or bath, put on a loose-fitting, comfortable, clean garment. You may wish to purchase a simple robe to wear just for your spiritual practice. This is a good idea, as it helps to set this time apart from the rest of your day. As you will only wear this robe for spiritual practices, it will itself build power over time.

Although bathing and wearing special attire will help to prepare you for your fifteen-minute Workout for the Soul, these are optional steps. The main thing is to develop the correct relaxed and open frame of mind in which to begin.

Removing Jewelry

One other thing is to ensure that you are not wearing metal on your body, particularly your hands or fingers. Metal attracts the spiritual energy you will be invoking and so will cause some blockage to the free flow of this energy. Some people wear a wedding ring or other piece of jewelry that they cannot or will not remove. That is fine; just remove what you can. I have taught dozens of healing classes with students who could no longer remove a ring or bracelet, and the healing power still flowed through them.

Preparing Your Mind

You are now ready to prepare yourself physically, mentally and emotionally for the journey within. You have set the scene; you are clean and your environment is purified. Now, you should start to prepare your mind to be open, free from worry and doubt, clear and expectant.

Read aloud one of your favorite inspirational quotations or aphorisms. Again, this is a personal choice, and I suggest that you change the aphorism you read from time to time as your own needs change. However, for the purposes of this practice, begin by reading aloud the following ancient Chinese aphorism from Deng Ming-Dao:

This is the moment of embarking. All auspicious signs are in place. In the beginning, all things are hopeful. We prepare ourselves to start anew. Though we may be intent on the magnificent journey ahead, all things are contained in the first moment: our optimism, our faith, our resolution, our innocence.

In order to start, we must make a decision. The decision is a commitment to daily self-cultivation. We must make a strong connection to our inner selves. Outside matters are superfluous. Alone and naked, we negotiate all of life's travails. Therefore, we alone must make something of ourselves, transforming ourselves into the instruments for experiencing the deepest spiritual essence of life.

Once we make our decision, all things will come to us. Auspicious signs are not a superstition, but a confirmation. They are a response. It is said that if one chooses to pray to a rock with enough devotion, even that rock will come alive. In the same way, once we choose to commit ourselves to spiritual practice, even the mountains and valleys will reverberate to the sound of our purpose.

The Power of Posture

Once you have read this aloud, be seated. Sit very quietly and still for a few minutes. If you are a student of Hatha Yoga, you may wish to adopt a simple Siddhasana or Padmasana posture on the floor. Sit on a cushion that raises the hips off the floor, taking pressure of your knees so that you are more comfortable (a buckwheat-filled cushion is an excellent choice as it is firm and supportive; however, any cushion will be fine). Alternatively, you may wish to use the Hatha Yoga exercise called the "easy pose" or Sukhasana. Sit with your legs facing forward in front of the body. Fold your left leg under your right thigh. Put your right foot under your left thigh. Keep your neck, head and spine upright in a comfortable position without being tense.

For most people, however, I would recommend sitting on a straight-backed wooden chair with the feet flat on the floor. Select a special chair that you use solely for this purpose. Also ensure that your chair or cushion is the correct height so that you can look at your altar when seated without having to raise or strain your head.

The Taoists preferred to sit in a chair when performing their spiritual practices, because it allowed contact between the soles of their feet and the ground or the floor, symbolic of the Earth. Sitting in this manner has the effect of grounding you as well as giving you power.

I have also performed spiritual practices in a comfortable armchair. This is not ideal because it is important to keep the spine straight and the feet flat on the floor. However, it can be done by sitting on the edge of the armchair, rather than sinking back into it. Other people prefer to stand while performing their spiritual practices, which is fine. The main thing is that you are comfortable and relaxed so that you can concentrate fully during the Workout for the Soul.

If you decide to sit, keep your spine straight with your head slightly tilted backwards so that it is in line with the spine. Sit away from the back of the chair, relax around your shoulders and place the hands palms downwards on the knees, with the middle finger lightly resting about two inches above the knees and the other fingers gently spread out. This spot just above the knee is one of our minor chakras or psychic centers. By placing the hands in this position you are completing a circuit in your physical body. This in turn enables the subtle energies to flow in such a way as to assist the inward-looking and contemplative state you wish to induce.

Kundalini and the Chakras

In spiritual practices the spine is extremely important and, as mentioned, you should keep this as straight and yet relaxed as possible. Sit or stand with the natural curvature of the spine, rather than being stiff like a rod, or bent over. The channel up the center of the spine, known as *sushumna* in Hindu terminology, is the channel through which the power of *kundalini* flows. Kundalini is regarded by the mystics as the "serpent power." This is the life force within us, and eventually we will all attain self-mastery by fully activating this great power consciously up the spine.

The kundalini power enables each chakra or psychic center to blossom and open fully in a state of enlightenment or bliss. When we enter this state, we become a "knower" or a Master. Instead of just feeling or believing that certain things are correct, we then know for sure. We understand more fully the great truths of the universe, the natural laws that affect us all, the eternal questions that have confounded all searchers for truth. In fact, at this elevated stage we are no longer "seekers for truth," we are now "knowers of truth." This is the aim of all mystics throughout the ages and the eventual destination of us all.

The chakras or psychic centers are like floodgates in our aura, which exists on a subtle level, around our physical body. Our aura is the subtle, egg-shaped envelope that surrounds the physical body and can be seen by clairvoyants as an ever-changing, multi-colored subtle body. The psychic centers exist within the aura and are connected to the physical body through the subtle nervous system, which is interconnected to the physical nervous system.

We have seven major chakras and many minor chakras, which I will refer to using the Western terminology of "psychic centers."

(See Figure 1.) These major psychic centers are (working down the body from the top): the Crown Center, the Christ Center (known as "the third eye"), the Throat Center, the Heart Center, the Solar Plexus Center ("the battery"), the Sex Center and the Base of the Spine Center. These centers are constantly taking in and radiating out energy on the level with which they are associated. For example, the Heart Center is constantly taking in and radiating outwards the energies of love. The more open and healthy our Heart Center is, the higher the aspect of love that is radiated and taken in by this center. The more we perform these practices, the more we will begin to open the higher centers so that inspiration and enhanced intuition, love and joy will pour in.

Breathing Rhythmically

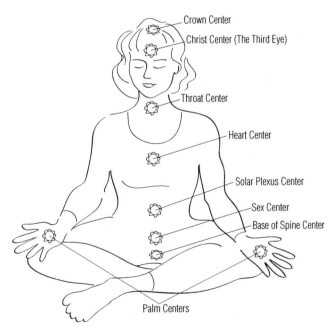

Figure 1.
The Psychic Centers (Chakras) of Man (using Western terminology)

Now that you have prepared your altar and have prepared yourself physically and mentally, you can begin to harmonize yourself through rhythmic breathing. Breathe rhythmically through your nostrils to do this. Correct breathing is extremely important, and you will be using breathing techniques more fully in a later step. However, rhythmic breathing is essential during all your spiritual practices and throughout your life. It will not only relax you but will also have the effect of putting you a more harmonious balance with Nature.

We all know the power that rhythmic motion can have, and many of us have heard the example of how soldiers stepping in rhythm on a bridge can destroy the bridge. The rhythm of our own breathing can also exert great power and strengthen our will, as well as allow more balance and vitality into the body.

To breathe rhythmically, inhale through the nostrils to a count that is comfortable to you, *i.e.* four beats or six beats, etc. Then exhale slowly and gently to the same count. Do this a few times until you can feel the rhythm vibrating through your body.

Remaining Quiet, Still and Receptive

Just try and open yourself up to the mystical vibrations you have already created. Watch your mind darting about from one thought to another. Do not try and control your mind; just allow it to be.

Keeping a Spiritual Journal

Set aside a notebook as a spiritual diary or journal in which you can note your feelings, inspirations and experiences. This will also be essential for your Workout for the Soul as you keep a record of your progress. Keep this book, together with a pen or pencil, easily accessible on your altar. At the end of each of the steps, write down any thoughts, impressions or physical sensations you may have experienced. Even if a thought appears insignificant, write it down.

It is a good practice always to make notes at the end of your spiritual workout, if you have the time, for during these spiritual practices you are stimulating your higher mind, the voice of the soul. Often insights and intuitions are more clearly revealed at these times. The more you write them down and take notice of them, the more clearly they will start to come to you.

Step One Exercises
Preparing the Temple

Day One: Find a suitable corner of your home to build your altar, preferably facing east. Select the altar itself; a small table or bookshelves is adequate. Now choose a chair or cushion that allows you to sit and look at your altar without strain. Select a beautiful cloth for your altar if you wish. Buy a notebook for a spiritual journal and place this on your altar together with a pen or pencil.

Day Two: Gather together any mystical artifacts and sacred objects that are inspiring and significant to you; remember to handle your sacred objects with respect. Introduce each of the elements onto your altar to bring balance. Consider setting up a green light to shine on your altar during your practices.

Day Three: Continue to build your altar. Ensure that you have a special loose-fitting robe or garment you can wear exclusively for your spiritual practices.

Day Four: Sit in front of your altar for ten minutes to see how it feels. At this stage, you may want to move the objects around. The altar should not only be visually appealing but should also feel right to you.

Day Five: Prepare the "temple of your soul" — your body — by bathing or taking a shower. Depending upon the time of day you choose to perform your spiritual practices, you may not always have time to do this, but make a point of doing it today. Wear your special robe and remove jewelry or metal from your body, especially your hands or fingers, if you are able to do so. Prepare your mind by reading aloud the inspirational aphorism given on page 26. Be aware of your posture. Keep the spine straight and the hands palms downward on the knees. Breathe rhythmically through your nostrils to a measured count, in tune with your heartbeat. Remain quiet, still and receptive.

Day Six: As Day Five. Practice for 10-20 minutes. Keep a record of each practice in your spiritual journal. Write down any experiences or feelings.

Day Seven: As Day Six.

Step Two
Refreshing the Soul

The invariable mark of wisdom is to see the miraculous in the common.
—Ralph Waldo Emerson

It takes a disciplined spirit to endure the monastery on Mount Serat in Spain. One of the fundamental requirements of this religious order is that the young men must maintain silence. Opportunities to speak are scheduled once every two years, at which time they are allowed to speak only two words.

One young initiate in this religious order, who had completed his first two years of training, was invited by his superior to make his first two-word presentation. "Food terrible," he said. Two years later the invitation was once again extended. The young man used this forum to exclaim "Bed lumpy." Arriving at his superior's office two years later he proclaimed, "I quit." The superior looked at this young monk and said, "You know, it doesn't surprise me a bit. All you've done since you arrived is complain, complain, complain."

Look at everything as though you were seeing it for the first time or the last time. Then your time on earth will be filled with glory.
—Betty Smith

If you were asked to give two words to describe your life, would you focus on the negative, as this initiate did, or on the positive? In this step, we will concentrate on the positive; we will practice developing appreciation. By doing so we will improve the quality of our life and enhance our Workout for the Soul.

We all want to feel better. We all have different things that make us feel better. We may believe that if we had a million dollars we would feel better. We may think if we were married we would feel better, if we had new clothes, a new home, etc., but the secret is to obtain the same mental state without the external things.

We all hear about people who appear to have everything, but live mean and miserable lives. Others seem to have very little and yet are filled with abundance and joy. This, of course, is proof that our attitude is not created by what we have, but by what we are. Our mental state does not own us; we have the power to change it if we wish. But to change a mental state, we first have to want to do it. Once we decide that we want a more positive mental state, then we can seek ways to develop one.

One way to do it is through developing positive attitudes such as gratitude, appreciation and thankfulness. I call these qualities "refreshments for the soul." By being appreciative and thankful we are helping ourselves to overcome the barren feeling that we do not have enough in our lives. By being appreciative we are acknowledging that we are fortunate recipients of life and its abundance, not victims of that mysterious thing called "circumstance." These qualities can be cultivated within us through inward reflection. They come as a result of wisdom, of experience, of realizing the precious gift of life and the reality of our higher selves. Once we learn to look deeper within ourselves, we will see abundance, tolerance and love — aspects of the God within — instead of scarcity and judgement.

Many people feel grateful for nothing. Others have nothing materially but feel blessed to be alive. It is hard for us to change, especially when we are bombarded by the media and society at large. The message we hear constantly is that the more we possess, the happier we will be. We have to learn to break free of this materialistic bondage and contact our inner world, which will teach us the truth and will show us how to gain lasting joy. In this step we will cultivate appreciation and learn how to see things differently.

Our lower self, working with our conscious mind, likes to continue its vise-like grip of control. Changing ourselves can be incredibly difficult at first because when we start to listen to our higher self, the lower self starts to realize its death throes are at hand. As a result, hundreds of excuses appear as to why we should keep things just as they are.

Our lower self is extremely clever and has many lives of experience. It will try and convince us that our lives are more difficult than those of other people, that we have much to complain about, that our relationships with others are inadequate and that other people are not very nice. Our lower self focuses on what is wrong and what is missing. Because we are concentrating on these negatives, they are what we see in our lives. This, then, has the effect of alienating us from others (who do not wish to hear our constant complaints) so that we become even more convinced that we are lonely, isolated and depressed.

We may honestly think that if only we had another $300 a month we would be happy. If only we had a prettier wife, a better job or more obedient children, we would find that elusive feeling of fulfillment. However, we must realize that our lower selves are never satisfied. We all hear stories of multimillionaires who suffer despair and loneliness as they go on their endless spending sprees, always seeking more. We constantly hear stories of drug addicts, sex addicts and avid materialists who are never satisfied, and who never feel they can have enough.

It is a vicious cycle that only we can break out of, through an inner change towards the abundance, love and joy that is our birthright. It is only through a change of consciousness and a realization that our greatest riches are within us that we will find the deep inner joy and love that we are seeking through our enriched spiritual life. Our efforts must be relentless and practiced constantly for us to succeed, but the results will be worth every ounce of the effort we make.

Gratitude and appreciation are essential parts of your Workout for the Soul. These twin qualities are aspects of our divine potential, and the more we manifest them in our lives, the more confident we can become that our divinity is beginning to show.

It is important to perform definite exercises until you are sure that your focus is on love, appreciation and gratitude. It takes 21 days of diligent practice to break a habit and several months of constant practice for a change to become internalized. It is, however, worth all your effort, for you can learn to summon joy and abundance into your life at a moment's notice.

Cultivating a Thankful Attitude to Life

Once you begin to appreciate the things you have and the people you meet, and see the beauty within all things, then you should give thanks. But first, take a definite step towards this goal by sitting down in front of your altar each day, as you did in Step One. As soon as you do so, give thanks to God (or however you feel comfortable addressing the Creator) for giving you another day of life. Say a simple prayer of thankfulness for the next 24 hours. Close your eyes and see these hours stretch before you, clean and untarnished, just as an artist regards a clean canvas. Realize that you are the artist. As such you can choose to paint your canvas of life with genius, love and inspiration.

In the next 24 hours you could help others, save lives or create a lasting treasure that could inspire generations of people to come. You have that power within you. Alternatively, you can choose to dab the canvas of your life with meaningless muddy hues that will depress you and cause others to look away in disgust. Every morning when you sit before the altar in your sacred space, realize that the choice is yours.   Contemplate upon this each day and afterwards read aloud these words (from Dr. King's book, *Operation Sunbeam: God's Magic in Action*):

Today is the greatest day in the whole of our history. Every day holds a promise for each and every one of us. There is a staircase at the beginning of every day that we can gradually ascend towards Heaven or descend to hell. Every day is great for every person in one degree or another.

Thankfulness to Nature

People in many of the so-called "primitive" cultures would not dream of going through a day without giving thanks to Earth for her abundant fruits, to the Sun for the warmth and life it brings, as well as for the food they eat and the stars that cloak the skies at night. In our modern civilization, unfortunately, very few people think of giving thanks to Mother Earth, who nevertheless supplies us with everything we need to live, love and gain experience.

Native Americans and other indigenous peoples realized that the Earth is a very evolved sentient life form, indeed a Goddess. She has protected and nurtured us for thousands of years. She has endured our hatred of each other, our disregard of the delicate balance of her nature, our explosions, dumping of radioactive waste — the list is awful and endless. She continues to protect us from the perils of outer space and provides us with a home suited to our needs. It is very strange that few of us give thanks for this, but instead take it for granted.

We bask in the warm life-giving rays of the sun and yet do not give it a second thought. It is a strange quirk of human nature that when there is a total solar eclipse, people will travel thousands of miles to see this miracle of nature. They will watch it in hushed reverence and be awed when the birds suddenly stop singing and a hush descends to herald in this majestic event. At these times of loss, we become suddenly aware of the power of the Sun and its life-giving rays. However, on every other day we take this great gift for granted and are even considered odd if we give thanks for this source of life in our solar system. It is a strange quirk of mankind that we tend to appreciate things when we lose them!

Many children are aware of the reality of the Devic Kingdom — the realm of the spirits of nature. As children, they have not yet lost their natural psychic abilities. Through their openness to life, they are still able to see beyond the limitations of their five senses. They see and play with the fairies and elves and often regard that as the real world. These nature spirits, as well as the mighty devas of the mountains, oceans, and winds, form part of the unseen but essential Devic Realm. This great aspect of life, just as important as we are, controls the weather and tends to the cycles of nature.

The mighty Devic Kingdom works in strict accordance with the laws of cause and effect and can only use the energy that is given to it by mankind. Earthquakes, floods, hurricanes and other natural disasters are not created by the storm devas who manipulate them, but through the wrong thought and action of mankind. If we, as a whole, were to send out streams of love, as is our birthright, then the devas could create the perfect conditions for our continuance.

If you do not believe in the existence of the Devic Kingdom, then you should try the following practice. Go out into the woods alone. Take off your shoes if you like, and feel connected to the earth. Be very open, and rid yourself of prejudices and dogma by allowing love to flow through you. Think of the beauty of nature and when you feel attuned to this beauty, say some prayers of thankfulness with love and every ounce of your effort and feeling. Then stand or sit silently and notice what you feel. Everyone I know who has tried this feels coming back to them the tangible love and blessings of the devas.

If we are not aware and do not see things, it does not mean that such things do not exist in realms beyond our limited five senses. Unfortunately, our current educational systems train us to develop and listen to our limited conscious minds, which tend to deny the existence of anything beyond their reach. If you reach out in an open-minded fashion to feel the existence of this wonderful kingdom of holy beings that works ceaselessly on our behalf, I believe you will find your proof.

My spiritual Master was very attuned to the Devic Kingdom and its work. This knowledge, combined with his incredible appreciation of Mother Earth, led him, through deep meditation, to devise a "mission" or activity that is global in nature and is performed regularly by the organization he founded, The Aetherius Society. This mission is known as Operation Sunbeam and is a very advanced metaphysical mission. I would like to briefly outline the mission here as a wonderful example of an act of thankfulness that has global implications.

Dr. King realized that Mother Earth is a highly evolved living being. It was this knowledge, coupled with his compassion, his vast knowledge of radionics (the science of the manipulation of subtle or spiritual energies), and the Law of Karma (the great natural Law of cause and effect) that caused him to invent Operation Sunbeam. This unusual global mission was devised to give back to Earth a "token" repayment — in the form of spiritual energy — for what mankind has selfishly taken from this living Goddess for so long.

Many of the ancient, so-called "uncivilized" cultures gave offerings and prayers of thankfulness to Earth, in the knowledge that She is a great living being who sustains us. Operation Sunbeam serves as a more potent and more technologically advanced way of giving thanks.

In Operation Sunbeam, vast amounts of spiritual energy are radiated to the Earth through certain psychic centers discovered by Dr. George King through his metaphysical knowledge and years of research. In order to perform this amazing feat, he designed and built complex radionic equipment, with the help of a handful of skilled initiates who will continue to perform this mission into the future. After years of work and effort, the first units of energy were given to Earth on September 14, 1966. Since that time there have been many improvements and over 500 successful phases of Operation Sunbeam have been performed.

Although the amount of energy given to Mother Earth is very small compared to what She uses, this gesture or token payment makes a difference. It has become an essential karmic manipulation on behalf of humanity. As such it has balanced humanity's karma to a great extent. Once we put things right on a spiritual level, our physical and other levels will also improve — with Earth and with all life. Hence the brilliance of Operation Sunbeam.

Most people now understand the concept of karma, _i.e._ that for everything we do there is an opposite and equal effect. However, many people teach that the results of this great law are inevitable. In other words, we create our own future, which cannot be changed. Dr. King was ahead of his time with his teaching that the future can be changed or manipulated for the better. This was the basis of much of his work and teaching, as he wrote in *Karma and Reincarnation*:

> We do manipulate our karma every minute of every hour of every day for better or worse. Every thought you think is a karmic manipulation; every breath that you take is a karmic manipulation for better or worse. If there is one thing that you do have complete and absolute control over at all times, it is your own karma. That should be taught in school before reading, writing, arithmetic, as it is far more important to children than reading, writing and arithmetic. This is the crux of all learning because unless you really know it, you will not advance.

Although only a rare, extremely advanced individual could invent such a magnificent mission as Operation Sunbeam, we all have it within our grasp to change our karmic patterns for the better every day of our lives. Giving thanks is one way to do this. Once we start on the path of thankfulness, whole new worlds of possibility will open up to us. Why? Because unlike the path of selfishness, which is by nature limiting, the path of thankfulness and appreciation has no limits. It is a path of awakening, a path of spirituality. The more we tread this path, the greater we will become.

Appreciating the Things and People in Your Life

Sit in front of your altar in your sacred space and spend a few minutes thinking deeply about all the things you have in your life: your job, home, family, friends, love, knowledge, experience, and so on. Think of all the good things, savor the feelings and keep these feelings uppermost in your mind and heart.

Now try and go beyond appreciation to enthusiasm for everything around you. Enthusiasm is infectious and is really an aspect of our divinity. Everywhere we see people who seem to be only half-awake. They glide through life, not really even seeing others, let alone appreciating them or feeling enthusiastic towards them. We know that we do not want to be like that. We want to be fully alive, awake and filled with abundance. With enthusiasm, we are on the way.

This leads to another point. When we see the sleepwalkers in the street and office, we tend to write them off as boring, dull and not worthy of our attention. Like us, however, they are sparks of God and one day, in this life or a future one, this divinity must be expressed. Perhaps your smile or kind words will help to wake them from their slumber.

As you begin to recognize the God potential in everyone you meet, you will begin to find that those people will start to reveal their goodness to you. If you seek goodness in others, you will find it, just as surely as if you seek to criticize them for their faults, you will find those in abundance. You already know this to be true. The difference is that you will now start to practice seeing this goodness in everyone you meet as a further step on your own path to inner fitness. Do this throughout your day during the coming few weeks and note down in your spiritual journal any special results that arise. I am not suggesting you be blind to, or unaware of, people's weaknesses, but that you focus instead on their positive attributes. The aim on this path is always to be aware of every pitfall and danger while maintaining a positive, spiritual focus.

Be Grateful for the Pain and Struggles That Life Brings

Gratitude for pain and struggle is extremely difficult for us all, but it is one of the most worthwhile practices we can perform. In the few moments you spend each morning in your sacred space, think back over some of the most difficult times in your life. Try and recall whether the experience left you with bitterness or with growth. If it is the latter, you are a person of wisdom, for this is the higher purpose of our struggles.

One of the most inspiring things is to hear about people who display strength of character in the face of terrible odds. You may think you could never be like that, but you can, because of the limitless power and strength within you. Just as the greatest among us have demonstrated the most noble actions and feats, so too can you. In fact, if you examine your life honestly, you will probably find that there are times when you have done this without a second thought. There are probably many times when you have put someone else first, have put yourself at risk, have expressed an opinion in defense of another, and so on. These are all seeds of greatness. In fact, if you can do something once, you can always do it.

The true purpose of life is very simple; it is to gain experience so that eventually through many lifetimes we return to the God source from where we came, as conscious Gods. Everything we go through is a result of our own thoughts and actions, and everything that comes our way can be regarded either as a curse or a blessing. Once we realize that, we can start to overcome our weaknesses and really grow.

To the truly wise person, the most difficult trial is the greatest blessing. That is hard for most of us to comprehend, but it is true. When we meet people who have really suffered in some way, we are often amazed at the understanding, patience and love they display. They often have an openness about them that encourages others to open up and talk about their own problems. A person who has really suffered can be the greatest teacher.

Remember to concentrate on an act of heroism, bravery, kindness or compassion at a difficult time in your life, and allow this feeling to imbue and inspire you throughout your day. Allow the greater thought to inspire and guide you always along this noble path.

Develop a Generous Spirit

This may seem an awful lot to achieve as you sit in front of your altar each day. However, all of these things are intertwined and are different aspects of a loving and gracious heart. Materialism teaches us to strive for results, for compensation, for recognition: all aspects of the ego, which will never bring true fulfillment or lasting joy. Spirituality teaches us to give without thought of any results, purely as an expression of the God potential within us. Once we learn to do this, then we will begin to feel joy. Only when we give freely with no expectations do we relinquish the ego's grip, to find another, more liberating world beyond.

Spend a few minutes thinking of the times when you gave freely of yourself with an act of kindness or assistance to another. Remember how you felt. Contemplate this feeling and allow it to flow through you like the energy that it is, the energy of love — not the personal, possessive aspect of love, but the higher, impersonal quality of love or compassion.

We are so conditioned by materialism that we may wonder why we should give without any thought of return. Society does not teach us to do this, but encourages us to have possessions in abundance. It takes courage and honesty to be aware of the conditioning that we all have and to break away from this. Only then will we be living in accordance with the higher Laws of Creation. We have only to look at the ebb and flow of nature, the sunrise each morning, or to experience the inevitable in-breath followed by the out-breath, to realize that this is the way we should function. This is the way we are meant to be.

Service as a Way of Life

Once you feel the opening of your heart and the flow of Love energy through you, you will start to realize more fully the connectedness of mankind. This is not just a nice philosophical concept, but a reality. In fact it is said that originally we all came from the same family, so that everyone on earth is a relative! We are bound together so tightly that everything we do affects everyone else on earth. We are constantly improving the lot of mankind, or we are contributing to making our future more frightening and limited. This is the "karmic pattern" of mankind that we constantly affect, and in which we share, no matter how evil or how saintly we may be.

One of the most important decisions we can make on a daily basis is whether we will contribute towards a future of peace and enlightenment for us and our children's children, or whether through our limited thinking and selfish acts, we will contribute towards the inevitable destruction of our race.

These are serious questions we all should face. By performing these exercises and the Workout for the Soul, with a heart filled with abundance, love and appreciation, you can help to ensure a bright future. This is the main focus of my book. It is designed so that you can become a virtual powerhouse and a radiator of Love. In time you will be able to send your Love around the world, bringing healing and strength to thousands of people you may never even meet. It may sound impossible now, but I promise you it is within your grasp.

Relax and Open Your Heart and Soul

During your practices, spiritual energy will actually flow through you. Although spiritual power cannot yet be measured as electricity can, it is as real as electricity and even more important. I would like to close this step with these inspiring words from Dr. King for you to contemplate during your quiet time each day:

> A rock is a living thing just as a mountain is a living thing. You try and climb a mountain when the Lord (Deva) of that mountain says you won't climb it and you can be ten mountaineers rolled into one, you won't climb it and that's it. First of all, you have to make friends with a mountain. All mountaineers know this consciously or unconsciously. You have to have a certain love for a mountain because it is living as all things are living, and they all respond to love. The Devic Kingdom responds probably quicker to love than any other thing. Their response is almost immediate. I don't need to tell you how animals respond to love, there isn't any doubt. Response is almost instantaneous with an animal. With a baby it is also, and with a grown up it takes a little longer. The younger a thing, the quicker the response and plants are just the same.

> So everything on Earth is living and everything will respond to this great power because it is part of everything. When you tune into love or radiate love you tune into part of the thing to which you

radiate it, whatever it is. You are no longer isolated from it because there's a link between that and you. It's like a tuning fork almost: you strike a chord and you link up one with another. If we could manifest this correctly, we would know about all things because here is a channel instead of an emotion. When once you start to regard love as an energy and not an emotion, then you start to understand it.

Step Two Exercises
Refreshing the Soul

Day One: Sit in front of your altar with spine and head straight and hands palm down on your knees. Be aware of your breathing and ensure that you are breathing rhythmically and deeply, through the nostrils. Offer a prayer of thankfulness to God for the next twenty-four hours of your life. Say this with all the feeling and love that you can. Next, think about the day stretching out before you as an artist does when regarding his or her clean canvas. It is up to you to paint your day with love, joy and appreciation — or the opposite.

Day Two: Be seated in front of your altar as before with deep, rhythmic breathing. Now think of Earth, Sun, Nature and the Devic Kingdom. Visualize each of these in turn and offer to each of them a simple prayer of thankfulness for their existence. Go out into the garden or the woods, if you can, and offer a silent prayer of thankfulness to all the spirits of nature. Wait silently with an open heart and mind and note what you feel in response.

Day Three: Be seated and breathe deeply and rhythmically. Now think of all the people you love and all the positive things you have in your life, and be thankful for them. Take this practice with you throughout your day and try and see the good in everyone you meet. Note down in your spiritual journal any changes in your relations with others.

Day Four: Be seated and breathe deeply and rhythmically. Recall times in your life when you struggled through pain and difficulty and overcame them. Think of how you have grown and strengthened through your struggles and be thankful for what you have learned.

Day Five: Be seated and breathe deeply and rhythmically. Recall times when you gave freely of yourself through an act of kindness or assistance to another. Remember how you felt. Contemplate this positive feeling.

Day Six: Be seated and breathe deeply and rhythmically. Read aloud the closing passage in this step (page 44) and then reflect upon it. End with a simple prayer of thankfulness.

Day Seven: Be seated and breathe deeply and rhythmically. Recall any feelings or thoughts you had during the week and note these down in your spiritual journal. Note down whether you feel any different after this week of spiritual practices and if so, how.

Step Three

Harmonizing with the Breath of Life

All the energy that is used in the creation of every cell in the universe is on that breath that you are breathing in.
—George King

Without mastering breathing, nothing can be mastered.
—G. I. Gurdjieff

Breathing is one of the most fundamental and important steps in our journey to inner fitness. The process of breathing is one of the great miracles of life, since without it we die. We enter and leave this world with a gasp of breath; in between, life is a continuous series of breaths. When we breathe, we live and when we breathe deeply and fully, we live deeply and fully.

The yogis and adepts from India knew that by controlling their breath, they controlled their minds. For thousands of years, Taoist Masters taught natural breathing to their students through Chi Kung, Tai Chi and other martial and healing arts. Students of the ancient Chinese art of breath manipulation, Chi Kung, practice disciplined breathing as a way to gain total control over their bodies and minds.

Because breathing is so fundamental, we in the Western world tend to take it for granted and don't think much about it at all. We feel that concentrating on breathing is like spending our precious time re-learning how to walk; it seems like a waste of time. In fact it is not. Most of us do not get the full benefit of our in- and out-breaths because only a small percentage of people breathe with the full capacity of their lungs. Centuries of bad habits, neglect and poor posture have affected our ability to breathe correctly, which in turn has affected our health and quality of life.

The most common mistake people make is to breathe too shallowly, using only the top portion of the lungs. This means that they are breathing too fast. The average rate of breathing is 12-15 times a minute and this is considered much faster than it should be. The ancient mystics taught that our life is measured by the number of breaths and that we could extend our life by breathing more slowly.

Correct breathing brings us so many wonderful benefits, including enhanced mental strength, more happiness, self-control, clearer sight, stronger voice, more dynamism, less fear and anxiety, exercise of our internal organs as well as better health and vitality through an improved immune system.

The best way to realize the truth of this is to start breathing correctly using the complete breath, which we will do later in this step. It is ironic that we spend so much time and money searching for external solutions to our global problems of ill-health and lack of vitality, while we neglect the potential of the greatest source of energy available to us — our breathing. While physical exercise, vitamins and minerals, balanced nutrition, herbal medicine, etc., are important to achieve and maintain good health, the starting point for us all is correct breathing habits. After all, breathing is something we have to do anyway — let's try and do it correctly!

The mind is by its nature unsteady and constantly affected by what we see, hear, feel, etc., every minute of every day. When we begin to concentrate our minds, we will find that our breathing automatically becomes deeper and slower. When we have bad news that causes us to feel sad or angry, we should notice that our breathing tends to become irregular, the opposite of the slow, smooth flow of the breath when the mind is calm. This proves that our mind and breath are interdependent. Each is unable to act independently of the other. Correct breathing gives us physiological and psychological balance. This is such an important fact that you should write down the following words in your journal for constant reference: *My mind affects my breath; my breath affects my mind.*

We are conscious of our thoughts and are aware that we are thinking. However, the Westerner's knowledge of the mind is rather limited. After all, the mind can't be dissected or measured, as the brain can. We are aware that something is going on inside, and we know that somehow the workings of our mind affect what we do with our physical body. We know that every time we move a limb or scratch our nose, our subconscious mind is mysteriously engineering the amazing feat!

We also intuitively acknowledge the relationship between mind and energy. We know, for example, that when we have lots of physical vitality, we also have greater clarity of mind. When we feel tired and fatigued physically, our minds usually follow suit and we feel we have "no mental energy." Just as our breathing affects our body and mind, the rhythm and rate of the breathing not only indicates our physical condition, it also helps to create our health and energy level. Breathing, then, involves far more than it appears to involve.

The quality of our inhalation and exhalation reveals much about our mental and emotional state. We have all experienced this link many times. When we laugh, yawn, gasp or sigh, our miraculous subconscious mind provides us with the extra energy needed for these different actions. Through awareness of our own breathing patterns, we can learn a lot. For example, we tend to forget and restrict our breathing when we are fearful or anxious. Our body does this naturally. Our subconscious mind automatically contracts various body parts so that the energy normally available is reduced. When we are really fearful, we breathe much faster and may hyperventilate.

Hyperventilation consists of taking quick, shallow breaths from the top of the chest. This can be the result of poor posture, excessive tension and trying to maintain the "flat stomach" that is a popular image of beauty. Our stomach is not meant to remain completely pulled in and rigid, but should be supple and flexible so that it can expand and retract as we breathe. In fact, correct breathing develops the stomach muscles naturally reducing flabbiness and developing strength and elasticity.

Our breathing pattern changes again when we are experiencing pleasant emotions. Then we automatically increase the length and depth of our breathing so that we take in more energy; this allows us to experience the good feelings more fully. The trick, of course, is to remain conscious of our breathing patterns, so that by breathing fully and deeply we can help to relax ourselves and overcome anxiety and fear.

If you ask most people the purpose of breathing, they will say it is to take in oxygen in order to sustain our bodies and minds, or words to that effect. Some may know that when we breathe too fast, we reduce the level of carbon dioxide in our blood. This reduced level causes the arteries to constrict and this in turn restricts the flow of blood throughout the body. When this happens, no matter how much oxygen we may breathe in, we will still experience a shortage of oxygen. This has the effect of making us tense.

These are obviously extremely important factors and illustrate why deep, slow and rhythmical breathing is so important. Deep breathing of fresh, clean air fills the bloodstream with oxygenated particles, which are pumped by the heart to every extremity of the body, feeding every cell and causing toxic wastematter to be consumed. However, even this is not the most important part of breathing, as the yogis have known for thousands of years. They call this aspect of breathing the "negative" aspect. The "positive" and most important aspect is the direct absorption of energy (prana) by the nervous and brain systems, without which they could not exist. This is why the yogis and Masters in the East taught correct breathing techniques, referred to as pranayama, which means control or mastery (yama) over the energy (prana).

During our regular in and out breathing, we draw in a certain amount of prana, but in controlled breathing, or pranayama, we draw in more prana, which becomes stored in the brain and nerve centers. Our body will then be able to draw upon this storehouse of vitality as, and when, it is required. The yogis and the practitioners of Chi Kung can channel the prana drawn in upon the breath to any destination of the body where it is needed at will, revitalizing and charging the area. This is the basis of self-healing.

It seems strange that, as prana is so vitally important, little is known about it in the Western world. The following is Dr. George King's brilliant explanation of this vital force:

Every breath we take, every mouthful of liquid or solid we consume, is charged with that vital force known in the East as prana. In fact, prana is the sum total of all cosmic energy. It is the energy which enables you to bend your little finger; it is the energy which, manifesting as gravitation, causes a passing meteor to be drawn into the orbit of a planetary body.

Without prana, there could be no motion of any kind and all cosmic activity would fade into its original state of dark, motionless potential; for prana is the energy which brings forth the realization of the original possibilities into the numerous phases of active manifestation which constitutes the whole of cosmic creation.

Prana is the life of the atom and the vitality of the most elevated inspirations of the enlightened saint. All creation revolves upon an energy axis of prana. Ten thousand words could be written about prana without describing it in its entirety, yet one word is sufficient for the thinking man. Prana is LIFE.

Although everything contains prana, it is in its most accessible form in the air we breathe. Even though it is neither the oxygen nor the nitrogen; it is the energy which vitalizes these for, without prana, neither the oxygen or the nitrogen atoms could exist but would still be an inert possibility in the mind of the creator.

Rhythmical Breathing

Begin this week's practice of Step Three in your inner fitness workout as usual, seated in front of your altar. The best time to do breathing exercises is an hour before eating breakfast, lunch or dinner. If you wish to do these after a meal, you should wait three hours. Food in the stomach places pressure on the diaphragm and lungs, making full, deep respiration difficult. The breathing exercises will also interfere with the digestion of food.

When performing breathing practices, posture is vitally important. Sit towards the edge of a firm chair, with your back straight, feet resting on the floor and palms downwards on the thighs. Resting your back against the chair, hunching the shoulders or rounding the back in any position compresses the abdomen, inhibiting the motions of both inhalation and exhalation. If you slump even slightly, active exhalations become awkward. You should do a little test by breathing in the correct position. Then slump forward. You will find that your inhalations become more labored, with your torso moving slightly with each one, making the exhalations more passive and slightly forced.

Begin by performing the rhythmical breathing, as mentioned in Step One. Inhale through the nostrils to a count that is comfortable to you, then exhale slowly and gently to the same count. Do this a few times until you can feel the rhythm vibrating through your body.

Rhythmical breathing helps to control the respiratory center that is located in the medulla oblongata, as well as other nerves. The center of respiration has a controlling effect on other nerves, so that the person who has calm nerves also has a calm mind. As you breathe in and out, keep the time of inhalation and exhalation the same. This will harmonize your whole system, the physical body, the subtle bodies, the mind and the tired nerves.

Nostril Breathing

Once again, remember to always breathe through your nostrils, not through your mouth. The former brings better health while the latter brings disease; it is that simple. Breathing through your nostrils offers protection to your whole respiratory system, as the nostrils include a system of filters. However, when you breathe through your mouth, the cold, dirty air goes straight into your lungs and the whole of your respiratory tract remains unprotected against cold and disease.

The only animal who sleeps with its mouth open is man. Sometimes you may have trouble breathing through your nose if your nostrils are blocked up. Before doing any kind of breathing exercise, it is essential to unblock your nostrils. Close one nostril with your finger, sniffing air up through the other one. Repeat with the other nostril and do this several times until your nostrils are cleared.

The yogis taught that alternate-nostril breathing is vitally important. We tend to breathe too much through one nostril or the other. The yogis taught that a person who breathes too much through their right nostril develops over-active and aggressive tendencies. The person who breathes mainly through their left nostril is far more passive. Breathing first through one nostril, while blocking off the other with your finger, and then through the other for several times each day brings balance and harmony.

Many years ago, I spent a week taking groups of hyperactive and epileptic children on vacation. They were quite a handful, as you can imagine! One girl who was in a very bad way, breathed with her mouth open, hyperventilated and often screamed and kicked in sheer frustration. I discovered quite by chance that when I sent mental healing to this child, she calmed down and her breathing became slower. Gradually her mouth closed. Of course, healing is the great harmonizer and brings balance. It did not occur to me at the time, however, that had the girl been taught how to breathe correctly, she could have helped to bring balance into her own distressed world.

Relaxation Exercise

On the question of balance, it is very important to remain physically relaxed during your spiritual practices, as well as to be mentally alert. Deep, rhythmic breathing will help to relax you, but you can also use this quick relaxation exercise with your breathing exercises. It really does work and can be used any time you are feeling tense and stressed.

Lie down to do this exercise if you can. Close your eyes and direct your attention to each part of your body in turn, starting with your feet and ending with the top of your head. As you direct your attention to your feet, tense up the muscles in this area, hold the tightness for a few seconds and then relax. Next, concentrate on your calves. Tense and relax them. Continue this process, working your way and up your body. When you have completed the exercise, concentrate on a feeling of relaxation for about ten seconds.

The Complete Breath

Most people use only a fraction of their lung capacity for breathing. They breathe shallowly, using a small part of the rib cage. Their shoulders are hunched, they have tension in the upper part of the back and neck, and they become tired easily without knowing why. There are many excellent systems of breathing exercises or pranayama available, and I give details of one such system in the last section of this book (page 151). However, in this workout, we are just going to practice and perfect the complete breath. This is sometimes referred to as natural breathing, as it is the correct and natural way to breathe. We will undertake this in the three phases that occur in sequence when one breathes correctly.

Mastering the complete breath will take time, effort and patience, but it is worth all your efforts. Do not feel that you have to continue doing the complete breath, filling your lungs to full capacity throughout your day with every inhalation you take; in time you may be able to do this, but initially let's start small. Just make it your goal to do a series of complete breaths each morning with your Workout for the Soul and any other time that you are able. Diligent practice really is the key here because it will take time for your muscles and nervous system to handle this new technique. Persist with it and eventually you will find that deep, rhythmical breathing will become habitual. Eventually you will find it more difficult to take a shallow breath than to take a deep breath from the abdomen; this is because deep breathing is the body's natural rhythm and what our body naturally wants us to do!

The complete breath employs various spaces of the chest, abdomen, back, spine and solar plexus. The three different phases of the complete breath actually form one complete movement. These phases are, first, the diaphragm breath; second, chest breathing; and third, high breathing. Any one of the three breathing methods fills only a small portion of our lungs. The diaphragm breath fills only the lower portion and part of the middle; chest breathing, the middle and a portion of the upper regions; and high breathing, the upper portion of the lungs. The complete breath uses all three of the above methods in sequence, as one breath. As we learn to use the complete breath, our whole respiratory system comes into play, so that no portion of the lungs is left unfilled with fresh air and, more importantly, prana.

Diaphragm or Lower Breathing

Sit erect, with spine, neck and head in a straight line. Relax your abdominal muscles. Breathe only with the diaphragm, extending it outwards. This is the main muscle used in breathing, the strip of muscle that separates the lung cavity from the stomach cavity. You can visualize it as the floor on top of which the lungs sit – the abdominal dome.

When the diaphragm lowers, air is drawn into the lungs and the abdomen is inflated and pushed out. (See Figure 2.) Do not bend forward or use your chest at all. Take a long breath while allowing the diaphragm to descend without raising your chest or shoulders. Keep your neck and facial muscles relaxed and try to keep your in- and out-breaths of the same duration. Retain your breath for a few seconds and then exhale slowly. Hold your chest in a firm position and draw your abdomen in a little. Lift your abdomen upwards slowly as the air leaves your body. Try this a few times until you have a sense of the duration of your breath, the amount of air coming in and the destination of the air in the lungs.

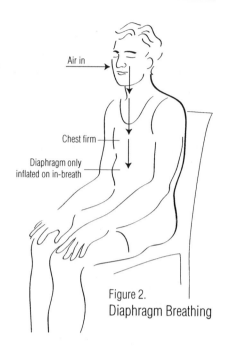

Air in

Chest firm

Diaphragm only
inflated on in-breath

Figure 2.
Diaphragm Breathing

Chest Breathing

Now, check your posture again and make sure that your spine, neck and head are still in a straight line. This time, do not allow your diaphragm to expand as before, and do not raise your shoulders. Instead, take a long, deep breath using your chest and ribs. As you breathe in, the rib cage should be able to expand outwards and move upwards. (See Figure 3.) Try this a few times, then place your hands lightly on your rib cage to feel the movement and to

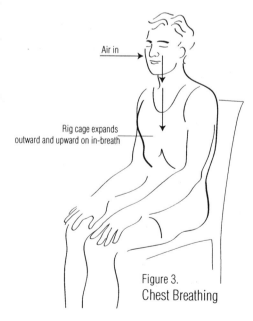

Air in

Rig cage expands
outward and upward on in-breath

Figure 3.
Chest Breathing

check that you are not moving the diaphragm. Use your inter-costal muscles (the layer of muscles between the ribs) to swing the ribs upwards and forward, pivoting them around their joints with the vertebrae. This increases the diameter of the chest, allowing the lungs to expand, pulling in air to fill the newly created spaces.

Again, get a sense of the duration of your breath, the amount of air inhaled, and where the air seems to go in the lungs. Compare this to diaphragm breathing. Alternate the diaphragm breathing with the chest breathing until you are comfortable with the difference.

Chest breathing requires more work to get the same blood/gas mixture than does the slow, diaphragmatic breathing. Since more work is required, more oxygen is needed, resulting in the need to take more frequent breaths. Because of this, more blood needs to circulate through the lungs, requiring more work from the heart. You can see, then, that how much work the cardiovascular system must do is directly linked to how efficiently you breathe.

High Breathing

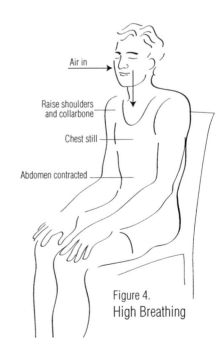

Once again, check your posture to ensure that you are sitting erect, with your spine, neck and head in alignment. This time, contract your abdomen, keep the chest and ribs steady and do not use the diaphragm or chest at all. Take a deep breath, but this time only by raising the shoulders and collarbone while the abdomen is contracted

Air in

Raise shoulders and collarbone

Chest still

Abdomen contracted

Figure 4.
High Breathing

and the chest is not used. (See Figure 4.) Repeat this high
breathing a couple of times just to get the feel of it.

Actually, after a lifetime of shallow breathing for most of us,
the top part of our lungs tends to be stretched more than the
bottom part, so that most of us do not need to concentrate on
developing this top portion of our lungs. We should concentrate
more on the other portions, and leave this part alone! Eventually
when the lower portions of our lungs are working correctly, the
top and bottom parts will automatically function together as they
should. Again, with this breathing exercise remain conscious of
your inhalation and exhalation. Maintain a sense of the duration of
breath, the amount of air coming in and where the air seems to go
in the lungs.

Once you feel you are doing this correctly and smoothly, use
the three methods one after the other. Compare each method,
experiment to see which one brings the most air to your lungs
with the least effort. The diaphragm breathing is the best method
of doing this, but if you find it is not the case, then you will know
that you are not yet using your diaphragm fully and correctly. You
should then continue to practice this particular method.

The Complete Breath

The complete breath is the main goal of Step Three. Once
you have prepared for it by mastering the previous three steps, do
this for five to fifteen minutes each day for the next week. If you
have a garden or yard, you may prefer to practice this particular
step outdoors. If not, open up your windows to inhale air that is as
clean and fresh as possible. I have heard people say that because
they live in a polluted city they try not to breathe deeply. However, it is even more essential to breathe deeply when you live in a
polluted environment because correct breathing consists of exhalation as well as inhalation. When we inhale correctly, we also
exhale correctly and by doing so we get rid of any stagnant polluted air that may still be trapped in the lungs. Correct breathing
ensures that the air in your lungs gets thoroughly circulated and
that the toxins are expelled on the out-breath.

You will have found that using each of the three parts of the complete breath fills only a small portion of your lungs. The complete breath uses all three parts in sequence as one breath.

Start by sitting up straight in your chair with your head in line with your spine. It is vitally important for your breathing exercises that you try and maintain a state of physical relaxation, especially around the neck and shoulders. Before you begin this practice, just roll the head slightly from side to side to stretch out the neck. Feel yourself become very relaxed in the head and neck.

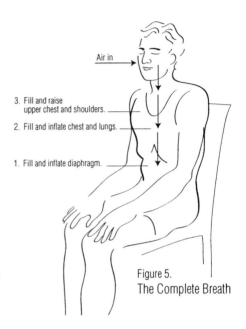

Air in →

3. Fill and raise upper chest and shoulders.

2. Fill and inflate chest and lungs.

1. Fill and inflate diaphragm.

Figure 5.
The Complete Breath

Now start breathing through your nostrils and inhaling steadily. First fill the lower, middle and high part of your lungs as above. Although these are three distinct movements, you now want to do them continuously. Retain the breath in the body for a few seconds and exhale slowly. Hold your chest in a firm position and draw your abdomen in a little, lifting it slowly upwards as the air leaves. When you have exhaled, relax your chest and abdomen. You may want to practice this important breath before a large mirror initially so that you can see your body working. Place your hands over your abdomen, so that you can also feel what is going on. At the end of each complete breath, your abdomen should be slightly drawn in.

As you practice the complete breath, learn to develop awareness of your breathing. You will find that as soon as you lose conscious control over it, it will tend to become haphazard and irregular once again. Once the breath becomes part of your awareness, you will begin to wonder how you ever managed to live while you were ignoring it. Also, try to maintain awareness of your physical body and avoid raising and tightening your shoulders. Instead, try and maintain a relaxed posture throughout.

Once you have incorporated the complete breath into your life for some months, you may start to feel stronger and healthier. We are conditioned to believe that to stay strong we must exercise our external muscles, but we tend to ignore the fact that our internal parts also need exercise. The complete breath will do this and so help all our internal functions from digestion to assimilation and elimination. It will revitalize the core of our being, and balance, harmonize and ground us, as well as feed our nervous system. Breathing correctly is like having a massage of our organs. We know how good it feels to have a regular massage; our muscles relax and we feel great afterwards. We tend to neglect our organs, though, becoming concerned about them only when they start to break down.

Apart from these benefits, correct breathing can retard and reverse the aging process. Although I want to stress that the highest motivation of this Workout for the Soul is towards spiritual growth and service to others — the noblest goal of all — I would be misleading you if I did not also stress the personal benefits you can obtain. That is one of the most wonderful things about these practices. Once we begin to express more of our soul potential and highest aspirations through spiritual practices, we may also experience many physical and mental benefits.

Aging affects us all. It is unavoidable and generally includes a loss of energy, strength and vitality. However, as we age, instead of relying on the physical body to lift and move things, we can start to utilize more fully this great power of prana that comes to us on every breath we breathe. As we get older, the deterioration of our physical body makes it more difficult for us to walk around and lift objects. We can no longer run and jump as we used to and sometimes it is even difficult for us to do simple things such as get up from sitting in a chair.

Lifting and Moving Using Inner Strength

The next time you feel so tired that you know it will be a great physical effort just to rise from your chair, take your thoughts inward. Be very still and visualize your mind going inward to your core, instead of reaching outward toward the room in which you are seated. Then once you are firmly rooted within, take a deep breath, open your eyes and lift yourself up using your inner strength and the power of the breath.

This is a technique used by martial artists. They do not slice their fists through a pile of bricks using physical strength alone. They use similar techniques of visualization and breath control, for they are aware of and have experienced contacting the great inner power within us all. At first you may not be successful, but try it again and again until you do feel a difference. Also use the same technique when you are lifting things or moving around a lot, or doing anything that may generally tire you. Note any difference you feel. When you start to feel a difference, you will know you are on the right track. The benefits of breathing exercises will no longer be a theory but a reality to you, and all you will then have to do is continue.

Yogis regard the physical body as the temple through which we live and gain experience. It was logical to them, and should be to us, to love and respect every part of the physical body. The complete breath is one simple and effective way to do this and also helps to prepare us for the Workout for the Soul.

Becoming More Aware of Your Physical Body

The yogis and mystics also taught that to be fully alive, one must be fully conscious. This applies to every step in this workout. Consciousness applies not only to our mental control, but also to the positioning of our physical body. This is particularly important during the breathing practice, as any tension will restrict the flow of prana. Once you have practiced and found your correct posture, remember to be aware of this at all times.

It is essential to keep your chest, neck and head in one vertical line. I cannot stress this enough. Do not bend your head either forward or backwards but keep it in line with the spine. Practice bending the head forward and see how tight the muscles at the back of your neck become. Also, keep the respiratory muscles of the neck relaxed. This will help to relax the facial muscles. When the facial muscles relax, they loosen their grip over the organs of perception (the eyes, ears, nose, tongue and skin), thus reducing tension in the brain and increasing concentration, balance and serenity.

Also remain fully conscious of your lungs. Keep them passive and non-resistant during inhalation in order to better receive and absorb the incoming energy. During exhalation, retain the grip of the intercostal muscles and the floating ribs throughout. Without this grip, steady and smooth exhalation is not possible.

Above all, sit very still for this practice and all the practices in this book. Since childhood we have learned to move, but no one taught us to be still! Sitting still is very important because the less movement there is in the body, the steadier your mind will be. The yogis teach that all twitches, gestures, scratches and wiggles of the body are caused by an undisciplined and untrained mind. When you start to watch yourself, you will find that the mind moves first, then the body follows. By the same token, the more the body moves, the more the mind dissipates.

Step Three Exercises
Harmonizing with the Breath of Life

Day One: Sit up straight in your chair with the spine, head and neck straight. Do this each time you perform your breathing exercises. Frequently check your posture and remain relaxed around the neck and shoulders. Practice the muscle tensing-relaxation exercise. Practice rhythmical breathing through your nostrils.

Day Two: Sit and practice the complete or natural breath, using the three parts of the lungs for five to fifteen minutes. Notice the effects afterwards.

Day Three: As Day Two.

Day Four: As Day Three. Try and be very conscious of your breathing patterns throughout the day. Remember to breathe correctly and as deeply and slowly as possible.

Day Five: As Day Four.

Day Six: Practice the exercise for lifting and moving using inner strength. Be more aware of your physical body. Continue these practices throughout your life.

Day Seven: Re-read the passage on prana on page 51 so that you understand it. Memorize the aphorism, "My mind affects my breath; my breath affects my mind." Note in your spiritual journal any effects of your new breathing pattern.

Step Four

Awakening Your Creative Powers

With visualization you are using tremendous creative forces; you are actually creating. If you visualize a flower, you have created that flower. In the mental realms, it exists.
—George King

Imagination is more important than knowledge. Knowledge is limited. Imagination encircles the world.
—Albert Einstein

In this step we will learn to enhance concentration, control the mind and awaken our creative faculty so that our Workout for the Soul can be far more powerful and our lives richer.

People often decry imagination as some vague condition that is the opposite of reality. As a child I found this difficult to understand. When I sat at the back of the classroom daydreaming while my teacher taught Latin grammar, my imaginative world felt far more vivid and vital than the dreary "real" world in the classroom. I happily created my own reality until the inevitable day dawned when I was kicked out of Latin class. Suddenly my daydreams were a reality as I was now in the colorful, lively world of the Spanish classes, which were deemed more suitable (in my stuffy school for girls) for those of us with "too much imagination" for Latin. Imagination was considered a lack of intellect and something to be avoided at all costs.

I later learned that Albert Einstein discovered his Theory of Relativity while daydreaming. This comforted me in my pleasant reveries, until I realized later — through a study of metaphysics — that his was undoubtedly a higher state of mind than that generally attributed to the daydreamer. Only when I first read Dr. King's words in his brilliant dissertation on imagination that, "Imagination is your only creative faculty," did I know there was still hope for me!

Some of you reading this book are already familiar with the fascinating world of imagination. Others may feel that this is not your strongest point. However, as an expression of the limitless potential within, imagination is the birthright of us all. People with logical, scientific minds can be far more creative, once they learn how to develop and control their imaginations, than some people who consider themselves "imaginative." This is because one of the best ways to develop this creative force is through concentration and focusing of the mind.

Concentration

Concentration is not an end in itself, but a method by which you can enhance your entire life. When you concentrate, you are using your will to control your conscious mind so that it can focus pointedly on an idea or object. Despite appearances, you can actually only concentrate on one thing at a time. If you think otherwise, you are wrong. Your conscious mind can fix on one object and then another and back again, but it cannot focus on any more than one thing at the same time.

First of all, you should understand the relationship between the brain and the mind, as they are not the same. Dr. King was extremely knowledgeable about this relationship and he explained it very simply. He likened the brain to a radio-receiving set. Your thoughts (or mind stuff) are transmitted in waves through space and detected by the tuner, which is your brain. The type of mind you attract to yourself depends upon the quality of your own thoughts and feelings at the time.

Most of us recognize this scenario of like attracting like. When we feel down and depressed we seem to attract ever more gloomy thoughts to us. This is in fact exactly what we are doing; our negative mental state attracts negative thoughts to us from the sea of mind. The way to change a mental state is to think differently. We can do this in many ways. For instance, when we study a piece of inspirational writing, we begin to attract similar inspirational thought waves to ourselves. This stimulates the higher part of our mind, known as the superconscious, and this in turn enables us to be more creative, inspired and intuitive.

Using imagination and creativity can bring success in many areas of life. Studies have shown that children who have a balanced "diet" of both left-brain, analytical activities and right-brain creative activities, such as art and movement, have better examination results. Research also shows that the most successful people tend to be very well balanced between the two sides of the brain. Forcing the left-hand side of the brain to learn more, to analyze more facts and figures is not the way to success, although it is typical of the unbalanced society in which we live. It is very sad that the latest trend in schools includes not only removing religious studies from the school curriculum, but also physical education. Instead, schools are cramming into the students more and more left-brain activities.

Gaining Control of Your Mind

Your conscious mind likes to regard itself as your boss and master. Because of this there is no point in dictating to it but instead we must learn to "reel it in" and control it. Treat your conscious mind as you would a fish. Imagine you are catching a fish on a line, where the first thing you do is let the reel go and let the fish take the line with him until he gets tired. Then you pull him in. Imagine that your mind is like this, because you are not going to control it by force.

The following exercise is one of the best ways to develop concentration and control the mind. Although it takes time and practice and requires patience, it is worthwhile. I suggest you practice it a few times before you go on to the other exercises. However, like most of the exercises in this book, it can be practiced throughout your life.

Sit down in front of your altar in a relaxed manner and concentrate on one of the items on your altar. You will probably only be able to concentrate on it for a short time before you start thinking about the laundry that needs to be finished, the grocery shopping that has to be done or the football game you want to watch. These types of trivial, distracting thoughts will tend to flow into your conscious mind as if from nowhere.

Now stop concentrating on the item, and just allow your mind to put these things before you, *i.e.* the laundry and shopping. It sounds surprising but this is what you should do. Just sit down and let these masses of thoughts come into your mind, then get up and walk around and detach from the exercise.

Later in the day, when you have the time, sit down and try this exercise again. Just allow the mass of different thoughts to appear before you. The key word here is "allow." Do not force, but just allow the thoughts to come up. Watch them. In my Master's words, "let the fish have its head."

Continue with this until your brain starts to seek direction and guidance, which it will after a while. Wait for this moment and then — you've got it! That's the moment when you can begin to control your thoughts. You have to understand this sequence. It is no good sitting down and trying to force anything, as many concentration exercises would have you do. You need to learn to relax into it. Taming your mind is rather like learning to tame a wild horse.

This exercise sounds very simple, and it is, but this formula will work for you if you practice it correctly. If you do this exercise regularly, you will come to a point where you start to have visions during your concentration exercises. However wonderful these visions may be, they should be ignored. My Master, who taught these mental exercises, explained why:

No matter what they are, disregard them as intruders. No matter how beautiful they are — you will see wonderful temples, golden Buddhas, and so on — they are intruders. You have sat down to concentrate on something else, not to have visions of temples and Buddhas. Disregard them — that surprises some of you, but it is true. If you don't you will fall for the big psychic trap laid for you by the conscious mind, because it's not easily going to give up control. It's not going to give its control up to the will and to the higher mind. The higher mind does not use force, always remember that. The higher mind has to be gently coaxed.

As you develop your psychic nature you will begin to glimpse a fascinating world. You will then be reaching beyond the limitation of your five senses and experiencing things you may have never felt or seen before. This hidden world can be beautiful; it can be frightening; it can be awesome and can appear more real than the material world around you.

While psychic development is an inevitable steppingstone along the path of spiritual advancement, it is not an end in itself. Some people, intent on reaching the higher states of consciousness, get stuck in the world of psychic phenomena. While there is nothing wrong in learning to develop your psychic nature, it is not the focus of this book. The purpose of this workout is soul growth towards the higher states of consciousness, self-mastery and service to all. The secret of success is to focus on our highest aspirations and let nothing pull us away from this.

Control of Sensation

There are many distractions to contend with on our journey within. You may find yourself troubled by outside noises, especially when you are trying to be quiet and contemplative. However, you can train your senses to ignore even these distractions. You already do this when you are reading a really interesting book and become completely oblivious to the noise of traffic, or the babble of television in the background. Eventually, you can become so engrossed in your spiritual practices that you no longer notice any outside disturbances.

The best way to start is with the following simple exercise. It helps you withdraw your attention from outer sounds and at the same time assists you in becoming aware of the sounds and feelings within.

> Sit in your usual spot in front of your altar. Listen to something in your room. It may be birdsong outside your window, or the clock ticking. Listen to it and give it your full attention for a few moments. Then try not to hear it. Do this again, but this time deliberately attach your attention to something else. This will take practice, but any exercise that helps you to detach from your senses will help you in your growth and development on the spiritual path. Try this until outside noises no longer distract you. Although an extremely simple technique, it may seem difficult at first. In time you will succeed, and it will help you to give full attention to your spiritual practices and so enhance their power.

Visualization on the Breath

By consciously producing a mental visualization while breathing, you can take your breathing practices up a notch. When you do this, your practice of rhythmic breathing and the complete breath will be far more potent.

> Before you start, read aloud Dr. King's explanation of this practice:
>
> *Don't be satisfied with the prana [universal life force] contained on the breath, but charge, highly charge the air before you breathe it by visualizing prana coming into the section of air that you are going to breathe, create a magnetic pull with your mind, throw out your thoughts and pull the prana into yourself mentally, as you do the deep breathing physically.*

> *You are creating a set of conditions with your visualizations,*
> *and if that visualization is done strong enough, with enough*
> *regularity, then that visualization must be brought into being.*

Next, perform the complete breath, using the three parts of your respiratory system as taught in Step Three, mentally pulling the prana into your body as you do so. Feel this charging you up with life and vitality. You are no longer just breathing in a controlled fashion. Now you are enhancing your breathing process through the use of your concentration and visualization. This is the next, more advanced stage, in your breathing practices.

Guided Visualization with the Five Elements

This is one of the most beautiful and popular visualization practices I have taught. It incorporates vivid color, as well as each of the five elements — earth, air, fire, water and ether. Because of this, it is extremely powerful and regenerating. If done correctly, this visualization not only recharges your batteries, it relaxes you at the same time. It is the next best thing to a dip in the ocean or a walk in nature. It will also assist you to correctly perform the more advanced visualization exercises outlined in the next step — mystic practices that are an essential part of the final Workout for the Soul.

One of the most beneficial practices we can perform is one that involves all the elements. Several of Dr. King's global healing missions are performed outdoors. He particularly enjoyed sitting with a few of his close students around a campfire, near water. Because all of the elements were present, this resulted not only in high spirits, but also, at times, high inspiration. As a student of metaphysics, you will learn to use everything in life and in Nature towards your own progress and the benefit of others.

I would recommend that you play gentle, soothing music while performing this visualization. This will help you to relax quickly into a quiet, reflective mood. However, if you find background music distracting, just sit in silence. Be seated in front of your altar once again and check your posture. Regulate your breathing and detach from your surroundings and any anxieties you may have. Then read the following visualization aloud. Alternatively, you may wish to record it for convenience. Read it very slowly and carefully, and enjoy it.

Allow yourself time to do this visualization correctly and relax into it. Make it an experience that you will want to repeat over and over again. Not only see the scene in your mind's eye, but also feel the breeze on your face, the water on your skin. Use all your senses. There are many benefits to this. You will be developing your powers of visualization, which will help you in your soul growth. You will also be actually creating this beautiful scene and will benefit physically, mentally and spiritually from the vibrant colors and from charging yourself with all of the five elements.

Imagine walking outside, through a door that leads into the country. The first thing you see is the wide vista of the country stretching out before you. Beautiful green trees rustling in the gentle breeze lead outwards to a wide valley, where a sparkling stream twists its way through the landscape. Reach down to the stream with your hands and splash the cool water on your face. Feel refreshed and uplifted.

Directly in front of you is a mass of multicolored flowers. The colors are like splashes of vivid paint in front of you: pink, yellow, red, blue, green and purple. See and feel these colors and bring them into you. See and feel the rich rose pink filling you, recharging your batteries. Brilliant yellow — feel its freshness stimulating your mind. Red — feel it giving you energy and strength. Blue — feel its calming influence. Violet — feel this uplifting you, inspiring you, with its clean, spiritual vibrations.

Now take a few deep breaths. Use the complete breath several times and feel the clean, fresh country air filling your abdomen and lungs, sparkling, cooling, vibrant and healing.

Now that you have charged yourself up, feel lighter of step as you walk down this beautiful, rustic country path. Feel the short green grass springing beneath your feet. Bend down and feel the Earth. Feel the power and strength of this beautiful home in space, the

Mother Earth. Feel yourself in touch with this power and strength and with the whole of Mother Nature. Really appreciate this and give thanks for her bounty.

You suddenly are aware of the beautiful sound of bird song, as if serenading you on this glorious, warm summer day. Now, feel the warmth of the sun as you raise your face upwards to this great source of light and life within our solar system. Realize that the outpouring of the sun's glorious energies makes all life in this solar system possible. Even our bodies are solidified sunlight. Everything we see, feel, hear and smell in this scene is too. Even the great pranas are sunlight on one of the energy planes or another. Feel the ether pervading all things — the fifth element.

Send your thankfulness to this great source of life — the Sun — and breathe in its dynamic energies. Feel its warmth as you return from this country scene, back through the door.

You are renewed, vibrant, uplifted, recharged, relaxed and strengthened in every way. Now take a few deep breaths and open your eyes.

Contemplation

There is a difference between concentration and contemplation. We all understand the importance of concentration, and we know that without it we cannot achieve very much. When we concentrate we use our will to direct our mind or brain. With contemplation, however, you lead your mind and then allow it to make its own deductions. Thus, contemplation is a more advanced state of mind.

When a person repeats a holy mantra, for instance, this is the highest form of prayer. When repeated it has the effect of changing your environment and your own vibrations for the better. Although you may not understand the meaning of the particular mantra, you will benefit by practicing the sacred science of mantra. If you were serious about your advancement, you might decide to repeat a mantra and concentrate your mind on this mantra for several hours. However, in contemplation you would force or direct your mind to repeat the mantra just once or twice and then you would contemplate its true and inner meaning.

You will see that contemplation is not an easy state to achieve. It takes a good deal of hard work and effort. We tend to think of it as one in which we just let the mind wander, but that would be a negative state of daydreaming or reflection, wherein the information that comes tends to be random. If, however, we have worked hard for many lives at concentration and contemplation, we may be able to achieve a true contemplative state quite easily. When I mentioned that Einstein was using a higher mental state than daydreaming when he discovered his Theory of Relativity, I was referring to the state of contemplation. He had worked hard to achieve this state either in his current life or in former lives.

Contemplation involves concentrating on something with the idea of learning about that thing. In other words, during that state, your conscious mind is open to impulses being sent to it from your super-conscious or higher mind.

Meditation is an even higher state than contemplation. During this highly elevated state, the meditator becomes at one with the object of meditation. This state of consciousness takes lives and lives of hard work and practice. Meditation is a very popular word, but its true meaning is not understood and very few people are capable of it. When most people refer to meditation, they are in fact referring to a reflective state. When the yogis and spiritual masters refer to meditation, they refer to the highest state of enlightenment available to us, also known as "samadhi" or "conscious death." Once this is reached, the meditator becomes truly enlightened.

For the purposes of this workout, it is not necessary to learn about true meditation, but there are several excellent sources that I recommend in "Enhancing Your Workout" (page 151), where you can find out more about this elevated state of consciousness. I would, however, recommend that you practice the contemplation exercise outlined in the next section (beginning on page 79). This will enhance your life as well as your Workout for the Soul.

Contemplation on Greatness

This technique, called *samyama*, consists of concentrating and contemplating a person or attribute that is noble in some way. During the samyama, or contemplation on greatness, you actually acquire an aspect of that attribute yourself. For example, if you feel fearful about having to speak in public, you may wish to contemplate a person who is extremely brave and fearless. You would consider the positive qualities of courage until you actually feel the qualities filling you. Certainly, if the person was great enough you should be able to do this. In fact, the greater the person, the better the results of this contemplation practice.

Do the following practice and, before you do, select the person that you will be contemplating. Make this the greatest person you have ever heard of, a person worth all your efforts, someone you really respect and admire and preferably one who is no longer alive. If you wish to think of a great Saint or Avatar, such as Buddha or Jesus, then do so. Perhaps it will be Hercules, Ghandi, Samson, Abraham Lincoln, Albert Einstein, Mother Theresa or someone you have read about who has really moved you. Ensure that the object of your samyama is a truly noble person, one who has qualities of courage, compassion and strength, worthy of your efforts.

> Sit down in front of your altar and feel relaxed around your neck and shoulders. Place the hands palm down on your knees and concentrate on the Complete Breath. Now think about the person you have selected, by name. Think about all the noble qualities that this person possesses until you start to feel inspired. At this point, you may actually start to feel the person. Select one noble quality of the person — preferably one you lack yourself — and contemplate it. You are now actually attuning yourself to this quality so that an aspect of it will flow to you. If you allow yourself, you will be changed and uplifted by it. You may wish to take another of this person's qualities and repeat the process.

This practice can really strengthen you, but do not make it into a personal thing where you talk to the person or try and relate to them in some way. Do not try and bring these high, altruistic qualities down in any way. Just leave them where they are and imbue yourself with them. We are all part of the whole and we all affect each other. We can choose to spend every day watching violence on television and attune ourselves to that basic vibration, or we can choose to study and contemplate the lives of the great ones in our history. By studying higher truths, we attune ourselves to a far higher vibration.

As we advance, so we raise and improve our vibrations. When we die our vibration dictates the realm into which we pass. In other words, we go to the realm to which we vibrate. We dictate whether that will be heaven or hell by our thoughts and actions, not by whether or not we go to confession. If you were a very gross, basic person, in most cases you could not exist on a realm with high, spiritual vibrations. If you were a kind, sensitive, good-hearted, noble person who had worked hard to help others, you would not, in most cases, go to a gross, basic realm. All of the techniques in this book are designed to help you raise your vibrations — if you use them.

Awakening Your Creative Powers

Day One: Sit in front of your altar and practice the Complete Breath. When the rhythm of your breathing is established, practice the concentration exercise given on page 68 to help you to control your mind.

Day Two: As Day One.

Day Three: As above, but now practice the Control of Sensation as described on page 70.

Day Four: As above, but now practice the Visualization on the Breath as described on page 70.

Day Five: As above, but now practice the "Visualization of the Five Elements" on page 72. Have music in the background if you wish.

Day Six: As above, but now practice the "Contemplation on Greatness" as described on page 75.

Day Seven: Practice the Complete Breath again, this time also with the "Visualization on the Breath." Keep a note of the effects of all these practices in your spiritual journal.

Step Five

The Mystic Practices of the Ancients

Behold the form of me, various in kind, various in colors.
—The Bhagavad Gita

He who would perfect his work must first sharpen his tools.
—Lao Tse

In this step you will learn practices used by the ancient mystics to assist them in their inner journey to enlightenment and spiritual power. Like the other steps, these mystic practices form an essential part of the Workout for the Soul. These visualization exercises were sacred and revered by the practitioners, who gave them, through initiation, to those who were ready. The practices were treated as precious jewels, and often recipients would have to undergo difficult tests to prove their worthiness and readiness to receive them.

Many stories abound in India and the East wherein students would walk hundreds of miles and undergo terrible privation just for a few words with a master or spiritual teacher. Sometimes the master sent away the desperate student to undergo further tests before the initiations would be given. This was the way of advancement. The mystery schools were elite places that practiced the ancient knowledge, where the gifts of wisdom and enlightenment meant more than the fame, money or success now prized so highly.

The necessities of this modern age are different. No longer does the aspirant or spiritually-minded person have to go into the wilderness and endure terrible hardship to gain wisdom and truth. The water-bearer, the symbol of the Aquarian Age we are now entering, pours the waters of truth freely to all.

As we plunge deeper into materialism, science and technology, the universal cry is for meaning. To the thinking person, the superficial qualities of outer beauty and fleeting success offer no lasting benefit or real value, spawning a growing trend to go deeper, to search for the soul qualities within. Consequently, we can now find spirituality everywhere, even in our local supermarket. Now, many spiritual texts and mystic practices are available. If we proceed with diligence and discrimination, we can find spiritual gems more easily than could past students of the mysteries. However, the key to unlock our own spiritual growth remains the same — practice, discipline and a genuine desire to live life at a deeper, richer level.

In the previous step you practiced concentration, contemplation and visualization. You will now practice advanced visualization, as well as practices involving the energy and power of color, which will further sensitize and prepare you for your inner journey.

Visualizing with Color

We are constantly bombarded with the energies of color, which have a definite effect upon us. It is now widely known that the color of the sky, our décor and our clothes all affect our moods. At the same time, our moods also produce color that surrounds our bodies and affects us as well as others.

From numerous studies on the psychology of color and how it affects the mind, the metaphysician knows that color affects us on all levels from the chromosomes and cells of our body to all aspects of the physical, mental, astral and spiritual bodies. The materialist sees a person as just a head, body, arms and legs. The metaphysician knows that a person in fact consists of an egg-shaped aura, which contains not only our amazingly constructed physical structure, but also many other bodies. These subtle bodies work outwards from the physical and range from the emotional and mental bodies to the high, subtle vibration of the spiritual body.

Science tells us that color is a mode of light vibration and, also, that matter radiates light. All matter, therefore, has a color vibration. Matter is continuously emitting rays and vibrations that affect us, so it is important to understand the different effects that colors have upon us. Each of the seven colors of the spectrum — red, orange, yellow, blue, green, indigo, violet — has a different rate of vibration. Each color has a different quality that can heal and strengthen and that can play a significant part in our physical and mental health.

Our brain tissues emit color radiations, infrared radiation and also radiation in and beyond the ultraviolet. Color also plays a large part in our aura, the subtle envelope that surrounds our physical body. Every thought, feeling and desire we have collects around us in the form of vibrating waves or rays of color. If our thoughts and feelings are pure, then the colors they produce will reflect this; otherwise they will be dark and murky. That is why a discriminating, experienced clairvoyant (a person who can see beyond the physical) will be able to see from the state of the aura and the colors it contains what type of person you are! It would also be possible to see from the colors of someone's aura, the mood they are in — whether they are angry, depressed or joyful.

Visualization exercises require us to imagine or visualize color. The purer the colors you can visualize, the better results you will obtain. You will find that once you understand the nature of color you can start to use it in your visualizations to produce instant "pick-me-ups" and to enhance your healing. For example, green has a wonderful balancing, harmonizing effect that can safely be used at the beginning and end of all healing work. In fact, using a green light bulb in the room where you perform your spiritual practices will also assist you. If you are feeling particularly stressed and do not have time to get out into the restful green vibrations of nature, you can instead bring the color into your life by wearing it and by visualizing it.

The science of color healing, known as chromatherapy, is a complex study that will not be covered in this book. However, I have listed the nature and properties of the colors below so that you will have an idea of the effect that each color has on you. This will assist you in your color visualization.

Green

This color lies at the middle or point of balance in the solar spectrum. It is the safest color of all. It balances out any imbalances in the body; it is soothing, harmonious, healing and restful. It is not by chance that many hospital rooms and clinics are painted green, nor is it by chance that we feel soothed and rested when surrounded by the green of Nature.

Yellow

This color gives the maximum light and has a powerful effect on the mind. The color yellow signifies wisdom and brings optimism and refreshment to the tired mind. It may be a good color to use when you paint your study, as it can assist you in your mental pursuits.

Orange

Orange offers a powerful tonic that has a direct effect in building energy. A stimulating color, orange brings self-confidence. Try wearing orange when you are feeling tired and depressed and watch the effect it has on you and others.

Red

This is even more stimulating than orange. Red sits at the thermal heat end of the spectrum and is warming and stimulating. It gives strength, courage and enthusiasm. If you wear red you may notice that people often remark on the color. Red has to be noticed, as it is bold and powerful.

Blue

Blue is a physically cold color with short, quick, high vibrations. Blue causes most people to relax and can combat nervous irritation. Once when I had a badly infected and swollen leg, I shone the color blue on myself, using a projector and a blue slide. I actually saw the swelling reduce before my astonished eyes.

Violet

This is the highest vibration of light with a high spiritual content. Violet can bring inspiration and is an excellent color to visualize in your spiritual practices. Later in this Step is the sacred practice of the Violet Flame, one of the most precious practices to use to prepare yourself for spiritual growth and enlightenment.

Many people instinctively use colors in their lives. Putting on a red dress when you are feeling depleted is wise, as red will energize you. Painting a kitchen blue is also good as blue has a sterilizing effect and is also used in color healing to treat infections. The best colors to use on an altar, or in a room where you will be performing your spiritual practices, are violet, purple, magenta or a similar color. Violet has the highest and most spiritual vibration of all the colors.

We can use color to assist us in our lives or we can use it to hinder us. However, like every other study, the science of color can be fairly complex and there are many factors to take into account. The above information just provides very simple guidelines that you can use and experiment with in your own life.

My spiritual teacher, Dr. King, devised a potent healing method in which he taught healers to visualize the healing energy as pure white because the color white contains all the colors. He taught that the body of the person being healed takes whatever color it needs from the white light being visualized by the healer to assist in the body's natural healing process. Your subconscious mind instinctively knows what you need and automatically takes the exact frequency and color of energy required for healing to take place. Another miracle of nature!

You can perform color healing every day of your life. First, ensure that you surround yourself with beautiful, pure colors, like the colors of nature, rather than dark, murky colors that affect negatively. Before you can perform the visualization practices in this step correctly and the more advanced mystic practices given later, you must understand the importance of color in your life. Once you understand the effect of different colors, you will find it easier to imagine or visualize them in your practices and in turn these will become much more powerful. You can begin, therefore, with this color meditation.

Color Meditation

Sit up straight in your chair and relax your body by regulating your breath. Read the following color meditation aloud slowly at first, until you have the scene set in your mind and can imagine it at will.

Imagine in your mind's eye, or picture mentally, a stormy sea of dark greenish blue. See snowy white spray dashing against the rocks. See the spray rising as the incoming waves shatter against the dark gray rocks. Then, look outwards and upwards and see a glorious rainbow spreading across the sky as beams of sunlight reach from behind the dark gray, threatening clouds. See the contrast between the dark, threatening ocean and sky, and the pure, delicate colors of the rainbow.

Hold this visualization in your mind for a few minutes and then, in your mind's eye, quiet down the storm. Spend a few minutes making the scene as calm as you possibly can. Part the clouds and lift the color of the ocean to a blue-green color, reflecting the beautiful blue of the sky.

Realize the power of color to affect us and understand that you do have the power and ability to imagine and create. Contemplate for a few moments the impact this can have on your life. You have demonstrated to yourself that you can create conditions around yourself. You can do the same in your own life, turning the negative conditions to positive ones.

The Sunbeam and Moonbeam Practices

The following twin practices also involve visualizing color and are designed for very specific purposes. These nature practices should be performed outdoors if possible. As you might imagine, the Sunbeam Practice fills you with the life-giving vitality of the Sun. You should do it when you are feeling depleted, tired, depressed, or generally lacking in energy. The Moonbeam Practice has the opposite effect. You should use it when you are overactive, stressed and uptight, when life is moving too fast and you need to calm yourself down. It does more than relax the physical body; it will also relax and calm you at a much deeper level.

The Sunbeam Practice should be used in the daytime, preferably in the morning or the early evening when the sun is not too strong. The Moonbeam Practice should be used in the evening. These two practices should be used when you feel you need them, but not overly often (unlike the Violet Flame Practice later in this step, which can be used at any time).

I recently performed the Sunbeam Practice on the beach. It was a glorious day, as it often is in California in the summer. The sun was warm and the ethers were alive with the sound of the ocean waves breaking and the smell of ozone. These were ideal conditions for this practice. I did not want to attract unwanted attention and did not have to.

> I stood on the sand and looked towards the ocean. I then closed my eyes, breathed deeply and rhythmically and then, using my imagination, visualized a beautiful golden sunbeam coming down through the skies and filling my head and body with the vibrant energy and life-giving power of the Sun.
>
> Using my mind, I guided the sunbeam down through me, out through my feet, and up the outside of my body and through the aura, back to the top of the head. I imagined myself as a golden glowing sunbeam and continued to breathe slowly and deeply, imagining that I was a sunbeam. I held it there for a minute or so, seeing and feeling my whole body and aura

charged with this power. When I had finished, I slowly opened my eyes and ended with a short prayer of thankfulness. Afterwards I felt refreshed and renewed. Now try this for yourself.

The Moonbeam Practice is done in the same way, resulting in a very different feeling and energy.

Visualize a pure, delicate, white moonbeam coming down and filling your head and body with its calming, ethereal presence. See and feel it filling your body and actually helping you relax. Feel your breathing become deeper as you do so. Again, guide the moonbeam out through your feet and up the outside of the body, as a beam of light. Hold it there for a few moments, charging yourself with this beautiful, delicate power.

The Violet Flame Practice

One of the most sacred practices we can use is the Practice of the Violet Flame. This ancient mystic practice was originally introduced to mankind by the Spiritual Hierarchy of this Earth in order to help us grow spiritually. This is a hierarchy of Adepts, Masters and Ascended Masters who live in retreats around the world and whose main task is the preservation and growth of spirituality on Earth. The silent, unsung work of these great compassionate beings, who come from all races, goes unnoticed by most. Without their tireless work to inspire and uplift us, humanity would be in a much worse state than we are now.

There are many fascinating stories throughout history of people with unusual gifts, talents and abilities who have advanced civilization in some way. A famous story is of the Count de Sainte Germaine, whose presence was recorded in French courts during the 18th Century for over one-hundred years as a young, vital man of outstanding personality and ability. Throughout this time, he never aged. He was an alchemist, mystic and philosopher who purportedly had connections with the Rosicrucian Order as well as the Freemasons. More importantly, the Count was also a prominent member of the Spiritual Hierarchy of Earth who had come among mankind to perform a specific mission to influence and help mankind at the time.

Mostly these advanced spiritual masters perform their work silently and without recognition from mankind. Unlike us, they do not seek approval or fame, for they are above such trivia. Being extremely advanced, they realize that fame and fortune are transient and insignificant compared with the lasting journey of our spiritual evolution. They are more concerned with the progress of the whole of mankind.

My own spiritual Master had an unusual physical contact with a female master who was a member of the spiritual hierarchy. He spoke about this fascinating meeting and gave details not only about the advanced technology they use, but also about the nature and position of many of their retreats. Unlike us, they are not limited by their physical bodies, but can live to hundreds of years in the same body without any deterioration.

I have given you some background to the Practice of the Violet Flame, so that you will respect and appreciate this wonderful mystic visualization, which I learned from my own Master. The Violet Flame Practice brings great protective benefits, including cleansing, purifying and strengthening the aura. A strong healthy aura will protect you from disease as well as from negative thoughts from others. Also, as previously stated, the color violet has the highest vibration of light and will help to open the pathway to the soul — the super-conscious mind, so that inspiration and high intuition can dawn.

You may ask, from where does this violet flame come? It is given freely and always upon our request from the Logos of Mother Earth herself. This great living Goddess beneath our feet who sustains us and allows us continued experience is an extremely advanced life form, far more advanced than we are. We are insignificant when compared to our planetary home. When we see the pictures of Earth from space we cannot help but be awed by her beauty and magnificence.

Our pathetic egos try and convince us that we are the really important ones, but this is not even logical once we realize that we depend completely upon Earth for our existence. Fortunately for us, her compassion is so great that she freely provides this mystic violet flame to come up from her very heart, the Logos of Earth, right up through our physical bodies and aura, every time we request it. This is a great gift as taught in the ancient mystery schools and now being made readily available to everyone. The Violet Flame Practice can be used by anyone, anywhere, at any time although, as it is a sacred practice, it should be used with respect.

When working in London and travelling by underground train during rush hour each day, I would return home feeling like a limp rag. I had been packed like a sardine with dozens of other people in a hot, clammy train compartment; some people were obviously sick while others were worn down from a difficult day's work. The atmosphere was tense, tired and difficult.

Violet Flame from Mother Earth

Often, when I got home, the first thing I would do was take a shower to clean the negative vibrations from my physical body. I would instantly feel better. Next, I would visualize the Violet Flame, which felt even better than the shower! Not only was my physical body then clean, but so too was my aura. This is a wonderful practice and the more you use it, the better will be the effects. As a spiritual gift, it should always be used with love and reverence.

Sit in front of your altar as usual, with your hands palms-down on your knees and your spine straight. Close your eyes and be very relaxed around the neck and shoulders. Practice the Complete Breath and allow the thoughts of the day to come and go until you feel detached and centered in the present. Then using your powers of visualization,

Figure 6.
Practice of the Violet Flame

or imagination, think down to beautiful Mother Earth, living silently beneath your feet. Feel appreciation and thankfulness for this great Goddess.

Now, with love in your heart, visualize flowing right up through and around you a beautiful vibrant violet flame. See and feel this flowing right up from the Logos of Earth, filling and purifying every aspect of your physical and subtle bodies. Take this visualization about 30-40 feet above the head and hold it there for a few moments, feeling yourself bathed and cleansed in the great violet fire.

At first you will probably find it difficult to visualize. Some people find color difficult to visualize; others may see it but be unable to feel it. The secret is to keep practicing, and have faith that when you request this cleansing flame it is indeed there. Have faith that your request for the violet flame is always answered. It may assist you to find a sample of the color violet and keep it on your altar. If you look at the color and then close your eyes and visualize the color in your mind's eye, that will help you. Then expand that visualization and see the color as a flame, coming right up from the heart of the planet, up through the earth, through your feet, through your body and up through your head. (See Figure 6.) It will probably take some practice, but it will be worth every minute you spend. You may also wish to practice this standing outside on the earth, either with or without shoes.

The White Light and the Violet Flame

This is an enhanced version of the Violet Flame Practice. While the violet flame can be used at any time to purify and transmute, together with the Practice of the White Light, it forms the perfect way to start your Workout for the Soul each day.

Once again, be seated in front of your altar with hands palms-down on the knees. Breathe deeply and evenly and close your eyes. Now, using your powers of imagination or visualization, see a brilliant beam of white light coming down through the ethers of space. Now, see and feel it entering your brain, purifying every cell of your brain as it does so. Bring this pure white light down through your head and shoulders and into your Heart Center, which is situated as a floodgate in your aura, in the front of your body, just in front of your breastbone. See and feel this brilliant light entering your Heart Center.

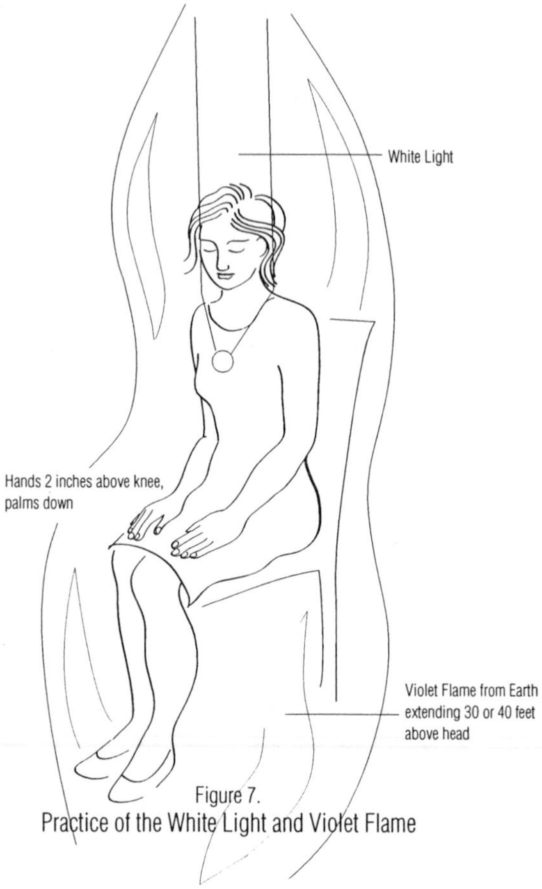

Now, once again visualize coming up from Mother Earth the beautiful violet flame of transmutation and protection. See and feel this coming up through your feet and legs and take it right up through your body, right up to about 30 or 40 feet above your head. Hold the visualization of the violet flame for about 20 seconds. (See Figure 7.)   You are now ready to start your contemplation, prayers, healing and any other spiritual practices.

White Light

Hands 2 inches above knee, palms down

Violet Flame from Earth extending 30 or 40 feet above head

Figure 7.
Practice of the White Light and Violet Flame

Practice of the Presence

This wonderful practice is an extension of the above two practices. You can use this every day of your life to benefit and strengthen you. You can perform this practice at the beginning and the end of your spiritual practices. However, for the purposes of this workout, you will use it at the completion of your practices. As this is an advanced and fairly complex visualization, we will break it down into nine parts, so that you can more easily follow the sequence.

1. Be seated, still and silent with your left hand on top of your Solar Plexus Center and your right hand on top of the left. Whether you are placing your hands over your solar plexus, or placing your hands on your knees while you sit, you are closing your "physical circuit." You are in the opposite mode from when you wish to open yourself up to send out prayer or healing energy. By closing your circuit, you are now ready to go within. Breathe deeply and rhythmically to instill calmness and inner peace and close your eyes. Be still and sit for a moment and feel at one with your higher nature.

2. Once again, use your powers of visualization — your creative faculty — to imagine and bring into being a pure, white scintillating light. See this coming down into your brain and feel it charging every cell of your brain. Take it mentally through your shoulders and into your Heart Center in front of your body, situated in the aura just in front of the breastbone (not over the physical heart).

3. Now visualize the violet flame coursing up through you from the Logos of the great Goddess

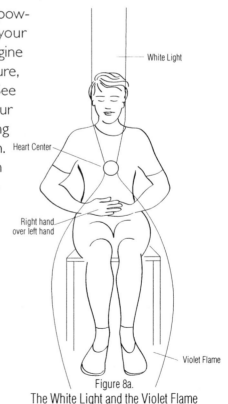

Figure 8a.
The White Light and the Violet Flame
Practice of the Presence, Part 1

beneath your feet, cleansing, uplifting and purifying. See this coming up and take it into the Heart Center also. (Figure 8a.)

4. Join together, in your mind's eye, the white light and the violet flame in the Heart Center, and take these two forces as one up through your spine at the back and out through the top of your head.

5. Now visualize above the top of your head a beautiful golden sphere. Know that this is the Divine Spark of God within us all. Although each of us is unique, because of our different experiences in this and former lives, we are actually linked through the Spirit or Divine Potential within each of us. We are one brotherhood of man, whether we like it or not. Although many of us on Earth have hundreds of lessons to learn, the Spark of Divinity within us all is perfect. This Workout for the Soul, together with all our spiritual actions and inspirational thoughts, assists us in the inevitable unfolding of this perfection. To travel those few inches deep within us is the longest journey we will ever have to take, but sooner or later, we must each do so.

6. Now visualize the wonderful golden orb suspended above you, like a miniature sun. With reverence and love in your heart, of-

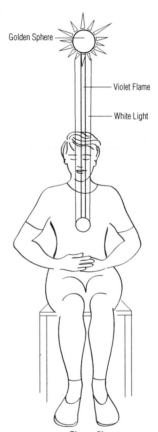

Figure 8b.
The Golden Sphere, White Light and the Violet Flame
Practice of the Presence, Part 2

fer into this golden sphere the white light and the violet flame. (See Figure 8b.)

7. Next bring down from the golden sphere its wonderful golden essence of complete spirituality. See and feel this essence coursing through not only your physical body, but also your subtle bodies, filling you with its golden Light of God Itself. (See Figure 8c.) Know that this Divine Essence is bringing you the wisdom, strength, love and understanding that you need in your journey through experience, back to God. Hold this visualization for as long as you can.

8. Complete the practice by saying out loud the words, "Great Peace, Great Peace, Great Peace. Thy Will, oh Mighty God, be done."

9. Finally, swipe your right hand once over your left hand in the Mudra of Detachment. (See Figure 9.) The practice is now complete and you are ready to continue with your day.

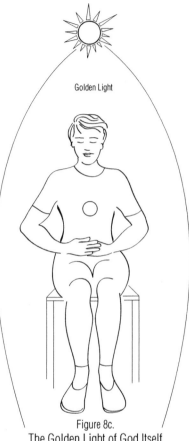

Golden Light

Figure 8c.
The Golden Light of God Itself
Practice of the Presence, Part 3

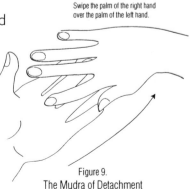

Swipe the palm of the right hand over the palm of the left hand.

Figure 9.
The Mudra of Detachment

The Mystic Practices of the Ancients

Day One: Decide to consciously introduce color into your life today and all week. Wear a red dress or a red tie today, and plan to wear green or blue another day. Look at the colors of Nature; the colors in your home and office and see how they affect you. Note down anything you feel from the different color vibrations.

Day Two: Be seated in front of your altar. Practice the Complete Breath. Now read and practice the "Color Meditation" outlined on page 84.

Day Three: If you can, go outdoors into your yard or garden. Practice the Complete Breath. Then perform the Practice of the Golden Sunbeam (page 85) to fill yourself with vitality. Remember to bring this down with your mind to the top of the head, filling your entire body. Then take it out through your feet and up the outside of the body and hold it there. Feel bathed and uplifted in this powerful golden light. If you feel you need the more calming energies of the silver Moonbeam Practice (page 86), then do that instead, during the evening hours.

Day Four: Be seated and perform the Complete Breath. Allow the thoughts of the day to come up before you and leave on the outbreath until you feel very calm and at peace. Then think of wonderful Mother Earth beneath your feet and say a silent prayer of thankfulness for her bounty. When you are ready, focus your mind. Using your creative powers, visualize coming up from Earth her violet flame of transmutation, right up and through you to about 30 or 40 feet above the head. Hold this for a few moments, or as long as you are able. (See page 88.)

Day Five: As Day Four, but also introduce the Practice of the White Light (page 89). First visualize the brilliant white light coming down, entering your head, charging every cell of your brain. Then take it down through the shoulders and into your heart center. Finally perform the Violet Flame Practice as above.

Day Six: Re-read the Practice of the Presence (page 91). Be seated and perform the Complete Breath. Be very still and reverent and filled with inner peace. Now perform the Practice of the Presence, making your visualizations as powerful as you can.

Day Seven: As Day Six. Perform the Practice of the Presence. Note any thoughts, feelings or experiences from this week in your spiritual journal.

Step Six
Building a Bridge to Your Soul

The only tyrant I accept in this world is the still voice within.
—Mahatma Gandhi

No pessimist ever discovered the secret of the stars, or sailed to an uncharted land, or opened a new doorway for the human spirit.
—Helen Keller

With every step you are building a stronger bridge to your soul. Your attitude, correct breathing, visualization and heartfelt prayers all help to make the bridge firm, solid and lasting. The firmer this bridge to your soul, the easier will be your journey within, and the more readily will your soul have expression. In this step you will use specific techniques designed to develop those positive qualities that are essential to the Workout for the Soul.

Faith

We will now examine the importance of faith and adopting it throughout our lives. Some people find it difficult to have faith in themselves, in external things or even in a higher power. These people often pride themselves on being realists. While realism is good, this word may be used to hide a fear of reaching beyond what can be seen and touched. Some so-called realists experience more obstacles and anxieties than those who have boundless faith and optimism, because of the realists' limited view of reality.

When people say they have no faith in God, or a higher power, it is because they cling to transient things and these form their reality. By its very nature, confusion and limitation must result. When one looks upwards at the planets and the stars, outwards at the beauty of Nature and inwards at the rich resources of our soul, it seems logical that there is a creator and higher power behind it all, very much greater than we are. Faith is not an empty thing; it is born from humility, awe and wonder at the perfection of creation; it is a stage after belief and before wisdom and enlightenment.

Faith requires us to listen to our intuition or to the wisdom of those whom we trust, such as a proven teacher. As there are many false teachers, listening demands discrimination and study, as well as open-mindedness on our part. We must first take the "leap of faith" to which scientists refer and then, if all the ingredients are there, we receive glimpses of a higher reality. You need faith to practice this Workout for the Soul, for unless you have faith that it will make a difference in your life, you will not even bother to do it. One of the aims of this Workout for the Soul is to strengthen your faith and make you more aware of a higher reality. The more you practice the workout, the more these glimpses will become a reality, and greater faith will be born.

Faith is a requirement for the evolution of humankind. A leap of faith always serves as the first step in any advances in science, technology, art or medicine. It is good for us all to use a healthy mixture of logic, discrimination, imagination, and faith in a higher possibility or outcome. It prevents us from being set in our ways, prejudiced or dogmatic — all those qualities that age us and prevent us from growing, and that stifle others.

Let's look at an everyday example of how having faith in others can assist them. The next time a friend tells you that he or she is going to start a program of exercise and lose ten pounds, don't answer from this position of prejudice:"That's crazy. You have never once completed any exercise program. You're not going to start now." Instead, be open-minded to the possibility of change, take a deep breath, make a leap of faith that it could work and reply in this vein:"Oh really, that sounds exciting. I know it's difficult to keep on those programs, but I'd love to help you if there's anything I can do."

It's a whole different approach to life. The first one is based on prejudice and your past experience, and will make you and others feel helpless and doomed to failure. The second approach allows for the possibility of change and is positive, helpful and hopeful. By approaching your whole life in this way, you will create positive change in your life, as well as in the lives of others. Your acceptance of the possibility of change taking place in your own or another person's life, becomes a catalyst for change.

It is good to be cautious and not take on more than you can handle. There is nothing wrong with advising other people from a position of greater experience and wisdom. But whatever you do, remain positive, have faith and follow it through. Faith is like a seed and, once planted, it will grow and flourish in our hearts. The benefits of faith are enormous. Unlike doubt, which erodes and destroys, faith regenerates. It is constructive in nature. Through faith, you can draw upon your inner strength and power in a balanced way. By having faith in the divine source within all life, you can help build strength in others.

I once knew a girl who was shy and timid. She so lacked self-confidence and faith in her own abilities that she hated being in a group of people. She feared she would be expected to express her opinions, which she felt were worthless. She tried to stay away from people and though she read books on positive thinking, she did not have the courage to do all the things she read about. To her, faith did not come easily.

She was, however, fortunate to have the support of a caring family and her first job, in a theological college, reinforced this support. There she was surrounded with kind, caring and intelligent people. One of the professors there encouraged her to become a teacher. His and others' faith in her abilities changed her life; she returned to college to train as a teacher and now has spent over twenty years teaching others — in colleges, through seminars, workshops, lectures and even on radio and television.

That girl was myself. I often think about how much I owe to the people who believed in me, had faith in my potential and were kind enough to encourage me.

> To build confidence and faith in yourself and others, for the next 24 hours, say only positive things about yourself and about everything and everyone you meet. Continue this for three days. Watch everything you say, and if you fall into bad habits, note down what you said and its effects. At the end of the three days, return to your former ways and watch the results. After several days of saying only positive things, you may find the approach you had before now seems negative and destructive. Try it for yourself. It is extremely difficult to do.

We all see things about other people that we do not like.; sometimes we feel compelled to express them. However, if you just treat this as an exercise of discipline for a few days, you may be surprised at how your perception of "reality" changes. You may also be surprised when you become more self-conscious   o f the effects that your words have on yourself and others. Being fully aware and fully conscious of our thoughts and actions is an essential step along our path to inner fitness.

Affirmation and Positive Thinking

Attitudes of faith, open-mindedness and positive self-expression are helpful for success in all areas of life. We have a natural urge towards growth, health and positive expression, and the Workout for the Soul will assist you in developing this. By the same token, you will gain far more from your workout if you approach it in a positive way, with balance and faith in the limitless powers within you.

If you find it difficult to have faith in a higher power, begin by having faith in your own intuition, which is your soul speaking to you. Things may not be easy but they will be right. You may still fail at some things, but if you keep following the "still, small voice within" you will be going in the right direction. If you find it hard to have faith in anything at all, you can change this negative state into a positive one through affirmation.

One of the most direct ways to express your soul is through the use of the correct affirmation, another essential aspect to the Workout for the Soul. Through your thoughts and words you constantly affirm things to yourself. If you are faced with a difficult problem or challenge, you may find yourself thinking that you cannot do it. This will function as a self-fulfilling prophecy.

You are undoubtedly aware of the power and creativity of positive thinking. You have heard stories about people beating unbelievable odds through the sheer power of their will and positive thinking. This is something we can all achieve by using the technique of affirmation.

When you affirm negative things, you are programming the subconscious mind in the wrong way. The subconscious mind governs all bodily functions. If you constantly tell it that you are getting older and sicker, then it will obediently carry out your instructions by making you older and sicker. The sub-conscious mind does not reason; it just obeys. It is extremely brilliant but it is not creative in that it just obeys what we tell it to do.

If you are an anxious type of person, you may find it difficult to stop worrying. It is extremely difficult to change your negative thought pattern just by a sheer act of will, more difficult than stopping an ingrained habit such as smoking. The best thing is not to try and stop, but to slowly introduce affirmations into your daily routine. These will have a ripple effect on your thought patterns. You will gradually find that the motion of the affirmation will knock your thoughts and words into better shape.

Dangers of Affirmation

Many people teach affirmations and you may already be repeating some. However, just as affirmations can change your life
for the better, so too can they be confusing and even damaging. I
recently read a book about affirmations and was shocked to see
the writer encouraging people to use untrue affirmations. The
author encouraged readers to affirm things to him or herself that
were downright lies. According to this book, even when you have
the flu, you should tell yourself that you are perfectly healthy, or
words to that effect. However, your subconscious mind knows
perfectly well that this is not the case. You should never lie to yourself, for a simple reason. If you tell yourself a lie, your obedient
servant — the subconscious mind — will try and program the lie;
this will cause confusion, and eventually your circuits will break
down!

One of the safest and most effective affirmations ever given
was the one written by Emile Coué:

Every day in every way I am getting better and better and better.

Although very simple, this is a brilliant affirmation that can be
used safely and successfully by every person. Why? By repeating it,
you will never lie to yourself. You are not saying "I am completely
well." Instead you are informing your subconscious mind of your
positive intentions to become better and are programming it to
carry out this instruction. Even though you may be sick when you
start affirming this, every time you do so you are assisting your
body in its natural healing process. Also, by repeating that you are
getting better and better, you are working to improve every part
of you — your mental and spiritual aspects as well as your physical
health. Finally, this affirmation has a dynamic and powerful rhythm
that will help to drive it into your subconscious mind.

By the same token, it is a waste of time to affirm to yourself
that you have no financial problems and that you are extremely
wealthy if in fact you are deeply in debt. This lie can only result in
confusion and, possibly, ill health. Your thoughts have the power to
change your life, but you must craft them with common sense to
get the best results. Again, you could affirm something to the ef-

fect that every day your financial situation is getting better and better.

Also, you have to work along with your affirmations. I know people who think that if they are affirming something, that is the only course of action they need to take. It would not make sense to affirm that your financial situation is getting better if you stopped working and went on endless shopping sprees! Affirmations work for you by becoming a part of you. But it is up to you to prove that you really mean them, by acting upon what you are affirming. In other words, we should not be hypocrites.

We are really a lot more like computers than we realize. Just as we love to blame our computer for the mistakes it makes, so too do we blame the conditions in our life or other people for all the bad things that happen to us. We have to take responsibility and realize that we generally create the mistakes and the bad conditions by our own negative programming! Affirmation is the best re-programming tool we can use.

I recently gave a talk at a one-day seminar on relationships. My talk discussed the relationship between man and Nature, the Earth, the Cosmos and God. The speaker who came after me talked about relationships with the opposite sex and told the students how to construct an affirmation that would guarantee their meeting the man or woman of their dreams. This kind of affirmation does work, as all affirmations do, but I would not recommend it.

One lady at the seminar had already had a bad experience with affirmations. She said she had written down all the qualities she was seeking in a man and affirmed every day that she would meet this person. Eventually she did meet the man and he matched up to her affirmation in every single way. The only thing she had not specified, however, was that her dream man should be available. As it turned out, he was happily married with several children! Another lady said that she had described her perfect man to be kind, funny, thoughtful, caring, etc., etc., and after affirming that she would meet him for some weeks, he appeared. However, he also turned out to be unemployed and impossible to live with!

It is always better to affirm positive changes within yourself than to request that positive things happen to you involving others. The most important thing in life is not that we have one relationship or another; it is not that we have this job or that college education. Rather, we need to unfold our own unique destiny in the way that is right for us. When we achieve this, all the right experiences, all the good things and people that are meant to come into our life will appear in the way they are meant to, in order to give us the experiences we need.

If you want to select only one affirmation to use in your life, then I would suggest one offered by my teacher, Dr. King. It is totally true and totally spiritual. It is the most positive thing you could possibly affirm and will bring you growth, advancement and expansion.

I am the Divine Presence which is creating perfection throughout my whole life.

This really is the ultimate affirmation. One of the best times to use it, apart from during your soul workout ritual, is when you are lying in bed at night just before you drop off to sleep. Although your conscious mind rests while you sleep, your subconscious mind never rests. This wonderful aspect of mind continues to perform its magic.

If the above affirmation is the very last thing you think before you fall asleep at night, then these powerful thoughts will continue performing their work, uninterrupted by extraneous thoughts and by the constant demands of your conscious mind.

Also, in the morning, at the time you set aside for your spiritual practices, sit down in front of your altar and affirm this affirmation out loud. Say it a few times until you learn the words by heart. Then say it another twenty times, counting twice with your fingers, so that you can concentrate fully on the affirmation. Say it with all your concentration and intensity and really mean what you are saying. The more distinctly and intensely you repeat affirmations, the greater effect they will have. Then rest for a few moments and write down any effects you feel or thoughts you have after this dynamic repetition of affirmation. Finally, aim to repeat this affirmation every day of the following week for at least five minutes.

Positive Thinking

The benefits of positive thinking are widely known. Like faith, it brings hope, optimism, confidence, joy, enthusiasm and all the positive, constructive qualities that indicate inner fitness and spiritual growth.

Thought has tremendous power. While light travels at 186,000 miles per second, thought travels instantaneously. Thought is very fine in nature but is extremely powerful. It can transform us or bring us down. Every time we think, our thought impulses travel to the cells of our body, and every time we suffer doubt, confusion or negativity our cells become weaker. This is why Eastern philosophy says that our physical body is an outer manifestation of our thoughts. When we worry constantly about things, it tends to show up on the physical body as deep lines or wrinkles.

Once we really understand how deeply our own thought patterns affect us, the next step is to learn to watch them, as taught in Step Four. Also, we can learn to clarify and focus thoughts through concentration; give them direction through use of our will; purify them through affirmation; uplift them through samyama, as also taught in Step Four, and through noble thinking and the study of truth. Then our thoughts become clear and forceful and our greatest friends. Slowly but surely the soul, or higher mind, will gain control of our thoughts and our lives. Then, we will no longer be blown like feathers in the winds of change. We will no longer be distracted by the whims of others, by our own doubts and confusion. Then we will be reborn, with the butterfly emerging from the chrysalis of our former self.

It is at the point where our thoughts are noble, born from the higher mind, that character is built. All the people who moved and inspired us throughout history had character. Character shone through their personality as strength, conviction, honor and integrity. It is the determining factor in victory. Once character is born — which can happen at any age — then we can add to our noble thoughts, by noble acts of kindness, courtesy and consideration to others. Then charm is added to character, making a magical combination that will attract to itself all the tools it needs on the journey to our destiny.

To counter anxiety and stress, which can hinder you on the road towards positive thinking, you need just two simple tools. The first is the ability to overcome negative thoughts and emotions by replacing them with positive ones. You can do this easily through vigilance and self-awareness. Just catch yourself the next time you are feeling depressed or confused and consciously replace that feeling by smiling and pretending to feel cheerful. If you find this difficult, read a passage from one of your favorite books until you feel better. Just replace the previous negative feeling, and then once again you are the master; you are in control. Do not doubt that you can do this because, according to the Laws of Nature, positive always overcomes negative; darkness cannot stand before the Sun.

You should also try and replace any habitually negative thoughts with positive ones. This is easier to do than just trying not to think them. Every time you see a habitual negative thought coming, try and turn it around so that eventually the positive one will become a habitual friend. For example, if you dislike getting up early in the morning and think to yourself, "I hate mornings," every time your alarm goes off, your mornings are likely to become more miserable over time. Each time you become aware of this negative thought, stop it in its tracks and turn it around. Try, "Great — another day is beginning!" or words to that effect, and see what happens. You may say you are not even conscious of your thoughts; if so, then now is the time to become conscious of them and how they are affecting you.

The second tool for overcoming anxiety and stress is mental relaxation. Try it just before you go to bed at night if you are feeling wound-up and mentally stressed.

Close your eyes and think of something very pleasant, such as a gorgeous sunset, the vast blue, foam-specked ocean, a deep blue sky framed with mountain pinnacles, a garden of sweet-smelling roses. Pick a scene in your mind's eye and imagine yourself floating in this beautiful scene. See the scene as vividly as you can and then feel the beauty of Nature pulsating through every cell of your body and aura. Feel cleansed and purified with the scene and become at one with it. Hold the visualization for as long as you like, in the healing power of silence. This will bring you mental peace and relaxation.

Harmony with nature helps us rest, because it is positive and the natural urge of our body is towards growth, life and evolution. Thomas Edison would come home after hours of work and lie down on his sofa, sleep for several hours and awaken perfectly refreshed. His wife said, "He was nature's man." Children are naturally more attuned to nature. They are good at being positive and happy. They don't even choose to be, they just are. As we get older we become conditioned to think that we should worry, that somehow worry is a sign of maturity.

The media try to teach us to be sophisticated, cynical and worldly. Instead, we need to get back to our childlike state. Practice being wholehearted, simple and enthusiastic about life. People are most often defeated not by lack of ability, but by lack of enthusiasm. Complexity drives our materialistic lifestyle and it is easy to get caught up in it. However, through this Workout for the Soul, you can find the simplicity within to help you drive a simpler, straighter, truer course through the stresses of life.

Once a doctor gave an unusual prescription to a business-man who always fumed and fretted and took work home. It included spending half a day a week in a graveyard. The doctor told him to sit there and think about the fact that many of these people were there because they thought as he did! They too thought they were indispensable; that time wouldn't wait. After a while the man realized that the world would continue just the same even if he slowed his pace. It was an unusual tonic given by a wise man – and it worked!

Study Truth

Norman Vincent Peale in his classic book, *The Power of Positive Thinking*, urges readers who lack confidence and faith to read through the Bible, marking passages related to courage and confidence and committing them to memory. You can use this technique with any holy book, because it helps to change your thought pattern. Choose a book that is sacred to you, whatever it is. Choose one filled with wisdom and enlightenment.

The study of truth also helps us to utilize our higher mind or super-conscious. As we rush through our day, performing the habitual things that are essential in our busy lives, we have little time or inclination to go deep. We have little opportunity to use our super-conscious mind to gain higher intuition and inspiration. Although Steps Seven and Eight in this book will teach you powerful ways to do this, another simple, quick way to become inspired is to study truth. If you travel to work by public transport, take an inspirational book with you to read instead of a newspaper or novel. Or perhaps you can read the newspaper on your way to work and the inspirational book on the way home, to uplift your thoughts after a busy workday. Always find time for even just a few minutes' study of a text that will take you deeper within. Your soul will rejoice!

Step Six Exercises
Building a Bridge to Your Soul

Day One: Practice thinking and saying positive things about yourself and others for the next twenty-four hours. Write down the effects and how you felt. Continue this practice for the next three days and see if you notice any changes in your life. Then continue to behave as you did before this and again note the difference.

Day Two: Affirm distinctly and with full concentration: "Every day in every way I am getting better and better and better." Repeat this several times until you have learned it, then say it twenty times, counting twice on your fingers. Then say it again silently, before you go to sleep at night. In the morning, note whether your sleep pattern was any different.

Day Three: Affirm distinctly and with full concentration: "I am the Divine Presence which is creating perfection throughout my whole life." Repeat this several times until you have learned it, then say it twenty times, counting twice on your fingers. Then say it again silently, before you go to sleep at night. In the morning, note whether your sleep pattern was any different.

Day Four: Practice being aware of your feelings and thoughts, and replace all negative states with positive ones. Continue this throughout the week.

Day Five: Practice the mental relaxation exercise of harmony with nature at night before you go to sleep (page 104). In the morning, note whether your sleep pattern was any different.

Day Six: Study inspirational, philosophical and religious works that are filled with noble thoughts. Mark any particularly inspiring passages and re-read them whenever you can.

Day Seven: As Day Six. At the end of the week, make a note of the overall difference you feel.

Step Seven

Prayer
The Song of the Soul

Prayer is the song of the soul and the soul wants to sing.

In the past, all religions have believed in prayer, but what they have not done is to go one step further forward to direct and discipline this prayer.
—George King

This is the most important step in your Workout for the Soul, for prayer is one of the most powerful tools for change that we have at our disposal. In this step we will examine exactly what prayer is from an energy point of view, as well as from a spiritual one. You will learn how to use constructive prayers for your own benefit as well as the benefit of others. Finally you will learn how to use prayer in a dynamic way to unlock your spiritual potential and help change our world for the better.

The Universal Language of Prayer

Prayer is a universal language. It is the common language of that universal religion — spirituality — of which we are all, by our very nature, members. Prayer transcends words, language barriers and different religious beliefs. Despite what many may believe, when people are faced with life and death situations, they almost always turn to prayer. When we are forced to reach deep down inside us, we find solace and help in that eternal "song of the soul" — prayer. One of the most powerful ways to express our soul is through prayer. Even people who profess no religious beliefs instinctively turn to prayer in moments of extreme danger.

When we learn French or Spanish at school, we spend years not only conversing in that language, but also learning how to conjugate verbs and construct sentences. We analyze, learn, practice and take examinations before being considered proficient. Prayer, being the language of the soul, is more important to us than a foreign language, but is generally left to chance. Although we may use prayer in our daily lives, many of us are never really taught how to pray.

What most people do not realize is that prayer, like everything else, can be learned. Just as you can become adept with your voice through study and practice, so you can become adept with prayer. Just as you can develop your muscles through weight training and your mind through concentration exercises, so, too, can you reveal more of your soul through prayer.

The Power of Dynamic Prayer

There are several different types of prayer. I spent many years in a mainstream Christian environment, attending "high church" Anglican services, with plenty of incense and prayer. I worked in a theological college, where the priests were trained to pray in a certain way using a certain style of voice. Although the prayers were, on the whole, positive, good, sincere and thoughtful expressions, they were not designed to radiate spiritual energy. In fact, neither the priests nor the congregation had a concept that they were sending out spiritual energy. Prayer was more of a personal relationship with God and there is certainly nothing wrong with that. However, the type of prayer you will be learning in this step is very different.

My spiritual teacher, Dr. King, taught this method of prayer as a means to radiate spiritual energy in a very potent manner. It is called "dynamic prayer." This radiation of spiritual energy is extremely important. Prayer energy is like a healing balm that can balance and change conditions on the surface of our world for the better, heal the sick and bring dynamic change in our own lives.

Prayer energy, love energy, spiritual energy — what you call it does not matter; it is a power just as real as electricity and far more important. We can channel this power from the infinite, universal supply. Through our prayers, we automatically channel this power; through dynamic prayer we do so in a far more powerful way. Dynamic prayer is one of the most potent keys by which to unlock the infinite powers within, to enrich your own lives and those of others.

What Prayer Is and How It Works

Prayer is a spiritual science. When you pray, you are not just saying words, but are also reaching deep within you. You are forming a connection with that spark of the Creator that resides there. Through prayer you can also radiate outwards the energy of love. Like the Sun, your soul wants to pour forth light, love and healing to all. Prayer enables you to do this. When this happens, you will receive more benefits in the form of enhanced health, greater dynamism and joy and increased mental powers, including intuition and inspiration.

Let us look at what happens when you pray, from a physical as well as metaphysical point of view. The floodgate in your aura, known as the solar plexus center, is the main storage battery of prana or chi in the body. When you pray, spiritual energy radiates through your psychic centers on the carrier wave of prana or chi. Remember that your psychic centers are constantly radiating out and taking in energy in order to sustain you on all levels. The higher and purer the aspect of love you are able to put into your prayers, the better results you will achieve and the more benefits will result.

Just like charging a physical battery on a battery charger, when you perform breathing exercises you charge up your own battery — your solar plexus center. This gives a greater energy supply for your prayers and other spiritual practices. Do not think, however, that by sending out this spiritual energy to those who are sick, or whatever is the object of your prayer, that you will deplete your solar plexus center — and your own health. Instead, as with all spiritual practices, the more you give out, the more you get back from the universal supply. We are born to radiate love, and the more we do so, the more vibrant we will become.

When this spiritual energy is released through prayer it goes to a particular person or situation. How it is directed depends upon a number of factors, including the words of your prayer. If you direct it to the victims of a particular earthquake, it will go there. Also, the power of your concentration, your intensity and your ability to radiate spiritual energy all assist in the effectiveness of your prayer. All the previous steps in this book have also assisted you in becoming a more powerful channel for prayer.

When your prayer energy reaches its destination it will bring balance and harmony, the same way as healing does. Prayer gives people extra power to heal themselves, help themselves, inspire themselves and motivate themselves. It assists, nurtures and heals. Your prayers can make the difference between life and death.

The Highest Form of Prayer — Mantra

Another very powerful form of prayer is mantra. You have probably heard mantra being chanted. There are even advertisements on television that use mantra as a sales tool. Mantra, however, is extremely sacred and should be given the highest respect. It is the repetition of sound sequences in the ancient language of Sanskrit. It is designed to bring about a change in our physical, mental and spiritual environment. When mantra is performed correctly it can raise your vibrations, as well as the vibrations of your surroundings, almost instantly.

Mantra is extremely powerful — the highest form of prayer. Although you can find books and people who will freely give you mantras to use, I will not be teaching mantra in this book for a very definite reason. An ancient, mystic law governing mantra states that you should not pass on any mantra to another until that mantra first lives within you. The person giving the mantra must be a master of this great yoga of sound, as my own teacher was.

This is not a man-made law but one of the ancient spiritual laws. It is a law of which many people are ignorant, leading them to repeat a mantra and then happily pass it on to another person. Although I have been performing mantra regularly for over twenty-five years, I still do not feel qualified to pass it on to you and, being aware of this sacred law, will not contravene it. A teacher of the spiritual sciences has greater responsibility than any other type of teacher. Such a person should ensure through his or her studies, discipline, practices and discrimination that the information he or she is giving is correct in every way. The price is the spiritual growth of students, and little is more precious than that.

I am not saying that the ancient, mystic teachings should remain available only to the spiritual elite. It is a part of the changing global consciousness that everyone now has access to the spiritual sciences, with numerous books written on these subjects, some of which are excellent. However, there are also some people "jumping onto the bandwagon" of spirituality who do not have the background and experience to call themselves teachers. You will see them teaching the popular message of self-mastery without effort. If one thing is impossible, that is. They offer to clear our karmic patterns for a large fee and give us the secret of instant bliss. I would advise you to always use discrimination. Generally, if something appears to be too easy, it is probably not valid.

I was taught by one of the best teachers of the spiritual sciences. His disciplines were hard but his teachings were of the highest standard. He never taught the easy way, but taught that we will advance through self-discipline, effort, hard work and, above all, service to others. This is not a popular message, but it is the truth.

This book will not give you a "quick-fix" to advancement, but if you practice your workout diligently, you can progress spiritually. If you are interested in learning mantras, and it is strongly recom-

mended that you do, you should refer to "Enhancing Your Workout, page 145, which contains information about places where you
can gain access to holy mantras.

Earlier in the book I remarked on the dangers of affirmations
and the fact that you should not affirm things that are not true,
despite what some people may tell you. This is a warning about
mantra, and this next section gives a warning about prayer. The
spiritual sciences are powerful and, as such, they can be used to
heal or harm. We must therefore ensure that we reap the wonderful benefits they can bring by performing them correctly.

The Correct Way to Use Dynamic Prayer

Before you learn the dynamic prayer technique, it is important that you understand what prayer should not be used for. Prayer
should never be used to try and change another person's mind. A
conscious act to change the mind of another person — however
evil that person may be — is black magic. In the world of the
spiritual sciences, we are no longer playing around on the surface
of life. The more we use our God-nature, the more we express
our soul and radiate spiritual energy, the more effective human
beings we become. The more effective we are, the more responsibility we have. The more responsibility we have, the more quickly
we can advance and evolve but, by the same token, the further we
can fall.

Just as many people are working to bring about spirituality on
this earth, so, too, there are forces of darkness or black magicians.
They use the same energies, the same concentration, similar methods of prayer and healing as we do. The difference is their motivation. While we spiritually-minded people want to help, uplift and
heal others, as well as advance ourselves, the dark forces want to
hinder spiritual progress and gain greater power for themselves.

There are only three kinds of magic (and by magic I mean
thought and action): black, gray and white. We see examples of
gray magic every day of our lives: lies, disrespect, pride, selfishness,

laziness, materialism and so on. By expressing your soul qualities, your thoughts and actions will become purer until anything impure will feel wrong and uncomfortable. "White magicians" are just people who frame their thoughts and actions in accordance with the dictates of their higher selves and so are living in tune with the great natural laws of the Creator. "Black magicians" consciously take the opposite path of indulging the lower self that wants more power and greater selfishness. The vast majority of people are not really consciously striving for good or for bad and therefore their thoughts and actions are mixed or "gray."

Bearing this in mind, it is important that you are always aware of your own motivations and make them as pure as possible. Once you get used to doing this, it becomes second nature, so that you are well on the way to self-mastery.

Strategic Prayer

If you hear the news of peace talks about to begin somewhere in the world you may feel inspired to send prayers to the peacemakers. Prayer will always be useful, but can be especially useful if used strategically. As the outcome of the war will depend to a large extent on the decisions of the peacemakers, strategic prayer is helpful.

Remember never to ask in your prayers to change the peacemakers' minds or the minds of anyone at all. We are here to love, to inspire, to heal — not to manipulate others. You should phrase your prayers in such a way that light, strength and healing goes out to the peacemakers in order that they may be guided by their higher selves to make the right decision. In other words, you should always leave the outcome to God.

On the next page is an example of the type of prayer we can safely use.

Application to Creator .. *Oh Divine Creator that is behind and within all life,*

Direction. . . . . *I pray that Thy infinite power and light may flow to all those involved in the peace-making process in [area of the world] at this time.*

Intent . . . . *So that they may be risen up to their higher selves. May they be strengthened, healed and protected at this time*

Faith in outcome . . . . *So that the outcome, oh God, may be framed in accordance with Thy Will.*

Thankfulness . . . . *I thank Thee, Oh Mighty Brahma (or whatever holy name you prefer) for listening to my prayer.*

As you will see from this, there is a formula for prayer, which you can use to construct your own prayers in a balanced and potent way.

Formula for Prayer

1. Application to Higher Power

You should begin your prayer by applying to God, or a Higher Power. It does not matter what name you use for God — Brahma, Jesus, Adonai, Allah, Divine Creator or Absolute. Just begin the prayer by reaching out to the Source of all Life, that which is behind and within all things, the highest to which you can aspire.

2. Direction

As with anything you do in life, it is important to have a conscious direction for your efforts. You should state at the beginning of the prayer the purpose and direction of the energy. By metaphysical law, the energy will then follow that intent and direction and do its work.

3. Intent

As well as giving direction, such as sending prayers of inspiration to the peacemakers, you should state your intention. After all, you are not doing this just to make the peacemakers feel happier, but so that they may rise up to their higher selves. You want them to make the right decisions, and are helping them to do this by sending them the necessary spiritual energy so that they have more inner strength, courage and wisdom to do the right thing.

4. Faith in Outcome

The ending of your prayer can take several forms, but it is good to express faith in the outcome of the prayer. Faith in a Divine Will enables us to detach from worrying about the results, and detachment is one of the keys to success in the spiritual sciences. You have rendered the prayer to God's will, you have delivered it with all your love and concentration, you have radiated and directed spiritual energy and can now have faith in the outcome.

5. Thankfulness

You may want to close your prayer with thankfulness to God or the Divine Creator. It is always a good thing to express thankfulness to all life. When you express thankfulness and offer blessings to a higher intelligence, the energy is returned in the exact degree that it was sent, but "colored" by the quality of that great Intelligence.

Now try reading the prayer on page 116 aloud until you feel comfortable with it. Practice it and think about the meaning of the words and the positive effect that they will have. Now read the prayer again with as much feeling as you can. Finally, read the prayer as if your life and the lives of others depended upon it. See if you feel any different. Note down any physical sensations, such as tingling in the fingers or hands, that you may feel. Spiritual energy will be flowing through you when you say these prayers. Some people are sensitive enough to feel this as a physical sensation, such as warm or cold.

Healing Prayers

You can use the same formula with healing prayers. You may hear of someone on the other side of the world who is sick and want to send them a prayer. This is good, for you should never resist the prompting of your soul. The more you follow it, the more guidance you will receive.

The life of the spiritual aspirant is not an easy one, but it is always a busy one! However, even though you request that healing power flow through you to the object of your prayers, you should again leave the outcome to God. A simple healing prayer may be phrased in this way:

Application to Creator .. *Oh divine and wondrous Creator*

Direction .... *I pray that Thy healing power may flow through me at this moment.*

Intent .... *To NAME OF PERSON so that s/he may be strengthened and inspired*

Faith in God .... *So that, if it be Thy Will oh God, s/he may be healed at this time.*

Thankfulness .... *I thank Thee, Oh Wondrous Parabrahma (or whatever holy name you prefer) and I pray that Thy Divine Will may be done.*

Make sure you address your prayers to a higher source and direct your prayers correctly. According to the divine law, it is equally important to be thankful for the outcome, no matter what that outcome might be.

However simple your prayers are, they will be effective. The above shows how to construct your prayers in the most effective way. By doing so you ensure that the outcome is in accordance with the great Laws of God, which are far more reliable than our own wishes and desires! If you do not wish to construct your own prayers, then I highly recommend two wonderful books of prayers that I use: *The Book of Sacred Prayers* and *The Twelve Blessings*. (See Bibliography for details.)

Making Your Prayers More Effective

I mentioned that the above prayers would be effective because of the way they are constructed. However, the degree of their efficacy depends upon how you, as the pray-er, deliver them. This may sound like you should resemble an actor delivering lines. In a strange way, you should. The more concentration, intensity, love, power and direction that an actor can bring to his or her part, the more effective he or she will be. When we hear a great actor, we just know they are good, even though we may not be theater experts. We recognize that they are better than average; they have the power to move us and to convince us of their intent.

When you learn to pray dynamically, you are not acting but are expressing the deep sincerity of your soul. However, there are many similar skills that can be learned and that will help your prayers to become more effective.

Prayer Mudra

Until now, you have been seated with your back straight and head aligned with the spine. You have had the palms of your hands relaxed on your knees. In order to perform dynamic prayer correctly, you should now raise your hands with the palms facing outwards. (See Figure 10.) This is what is called "the prayer mudra," the correct hand sign for prayer. Raising your hands like this allows spiritual energy to flow outwards from not only the heart center (the psychic center just in front of the breastbone), but also from the important psychic centers that exist in the palms of your hands. My master used to refer to the hands as our "spiritual guns" in that you can shoot out or radiate energy from them.

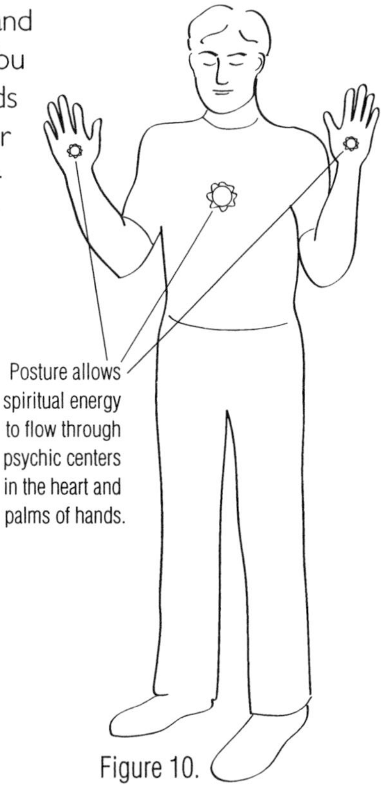

Posture allows spiritual energy to flow through psychic centers in the heart and palms of hands.

Figure 10.
Posture for Dynamic Prayer (Prayer Mudra)

An example of this is when you shake hands with someone and instantly feel depleted. In effect you are placing an important psychic center of yours — your palm centers — over the psychic center in the palm of the stranger's hand. If that person is depleted and fatigued, their body will draw energy from yours, causing you to feel the same way. In nature, the strong automatically give to the weak. This is the way of healing and the way of life.

If you wish to proactively protect yourself from depletion, you should try consciously directing energy, as a white light, from your hand as you shake hands with other people. This way you will help to charge them up with energy and you will protect yourself from depletion at the same time.

A similar thing happens when you visit a crowded public place, such as an art gallery or a museum. If you are a strong, magnetic person yourself, you may feel yourself being depleted as those around you unconsciously pull the energy from your psychic centers. When you are visiting such places, it helps to practice the Violet Flame Practice as described in Step Five.

Once you raise your hands in the prayer position, you can then start to visualize spiritual energy as a white light leaving the psychic centers of your hands and your heart center. You are then radiating spiritual energy and can direct this energy to the object of your prayer. At first this will feel strange, especially to those who have been brought up in a Christian environment, where we are usually taught to place the palms of our hands together in front of us.

The conventional Christian posture of prayer is in fact a mudra (hand-sign) of blessing. By placing hands together over the heart center, you are virtually

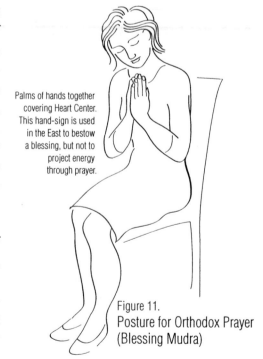

Palms of hands together covering Heart Center. This hand-sign is used in the East to bestow a blessing, but not to project energy through prayer.

Figure 11.
Posture for Orthodox Prayer
(Blessing Mudra)

blocking these centers off and creating a circuit in your body. This has the effect of containing the energies within your aura instead of sending them out. (See Figure 11.) If you bow in front of someone with your hands like this, you are directing the energy to them — as a blessing. It is certainly not the best hand position to use when sending out spiritual energy through prayer. I must stress that every prayer said from a sincere heart will be effective. However, the more tools we use to perfect our prayers, the more effective they will be. In this way, prayer is no different than anything else.

The Ingredients

Besides the formula for constructing effective prayer, a number of ingredients can make your prayers more powerful. The aim is to use every aspect of your physical, mental and spiritual strength when praying dynamically.

1. Posture

Once you have learned the correct posture, you should use it every time you pray. At first you may find that you stiffen around the neck and shoulders. You should try and be conscious of this and always relax yourself as much as you can. Remember to breathe deeply and rhythmically. It is said that the deeper you breathe, the deeper you think.

You may find that your arms start to ache after a few minutes. I have been praying this way for many years and can now keep my hands raised in this position for over an hour without resting. It is just a question of practice, like anything else. Any tension in the body presents a blockage for spiritual energy to flow freely. The goal is to remain as physically relaxed and mentally alert as possible throughout your spiritual practices.

You should make a note in your spiritual journal as to how you feel when performing this posture. Many people say that they find it very liberating and that they can instantly feel energy flowing outwards from their raised hands.

2. Concentration and Focus

As discussed previously, concentration is the key to success in all our endeavors. With prayer, you are concentrating on visualizing the energy flowing outwards from the palms of your hands and your heart center. Visualize this energy of love as a very pure and powerful white beam of light radiating out from you. Then read aloud your chosen prayer. Because your hands are raised, you may want to write out the prayer in large letters and prop it up on your altar in front of you where you can see it, until you can memorize the prayer. Read one of the above prayers, or one of your own favorites.

There is nothing wrong with asking for strength, healing and guidance for yourself and, in fact, you should do this whenever you need to. However, service to others is the most important thing for our own spiritual progress as well as that of others. Unlike the dozens of books available that teach us how to help ourselves, how to gain strength, confidence, success and prosperity, this book shows that these qualities are only by-products along the way to spiritual growth. The need at this time, as we move from the Piscean Age to the Aquarian Age, is to develop a consciousness of love and compassion for all life. When our thoughts, actions, prayers and healing are directed outwards in this way, then this is the most effective Workout for the Soul.

Concentrate on the words of the healing prayer that follows until you really begin to feel them. Learn this prayer by heart so that after a while it will start to live within you. When this happens, the results of your prayer will be greatly enhanced. (Note: Instead of Brahma, you may use another Holy name to begin the prayer.)

Healing Prayer

Oh Mighty Brahma
I stand before Thee now in all humility
And ask at this time that I may be filled with
Thy infinite Love and Strength.
I ask that I may be a channel for Thy healing power
To flow through me now in a great stream of Love
To all those who are sick and suffering at this time.
May these ones be risen upwards into Thy Divine embrace,
So that they may be strengthened by this.
May they be healed at this time, if it be Thy will.
Oh Wondrous God, I thank Thee for listening to my prayer.
And pray that Thy will may be done.

3. Love and Reverence

Read the prayer out loud several times until you understand and feel it. Then you need to condition it with your deepest feeling, love and compassion. Something that I have found works when I have taught classes on prayer is to ask that you first remember a time when you felt a deep love in your heart. It may have been for your child, your spouse, your pet, a plant, someone who was sick — whoever it was for, recall this feeling until you can physically feel it touching and moving your heart. Remember that love can be generated and created by us and that our natural state is as radiators of love.

Once you start to feel love, then imagine or visualize it leaving you and flowing outwards from your heart center to the world as a whole. Imagine this love as a pure, vibrant white light flowing out like a strong beam from your heart center. Maintain this feeling of deep compassion for as long as you can. Once you feel able to do this, raise your hands in the prayer position and also visualize the white light flowing from the centers in the palms of your hands.

Concentrate on feeling love energy radiating from you. Remember that the power really is actually flowing through you. In effect, you resemble a channel for this power that flows freely throughout Creation. Some people feel it as a river of uplifting power flowing through them rather like a stream of water. Once you have established that flow, then pick up the prayer and read it again, with all of the heartfelt feeling you can muster. Really mean the words. My Master was always urging us not to pay lip service to the words of our prayers but instead to throw every ounce of our deepest feeling into them.

4. Intensity

Many students I have taken through prayer classes over the years are quite shy, not very articulate people. It is difficult for them to even get up and pray in public, as this is something they have never done before. However, once we break through the initial barriers, everyone finds this to be an enjoyable thing. One of the most enjoyable and creative activities is to allow expression to our higher natures through prayer and to allow "our souls to sing."

I started teaching prayer in England, where people are known to be reserved and often dislike expressing themselves in public. I find it sad that many people go through life without experiencing the sheer joy of dynamic prayer. Through prayer, you can put the fullest intensity and love of which you are capable into expression. Many actors and singers learn to do this, but the majority of people have little opportunity. However, my Master believed that everyone is capable of deep feeling; he jokingly suggested that you really anger and annoy someone and see what happens! It is strange that for many of us the deepest feeling we express is our anger! This is why dynamic prayer is so important for us all to learn and practice.

Many of us are also conditioned to believe that it is somehow wrong to put expression into a prayer. We hear the priests in the Church saying prayer in monotonous voices, so that this seems the acceptable way to pray. On the spiritual path, we constantly have to break away from conditioning and allow "our souls to sing" freely. The rewards will not only come back to us, but will flow out to our spiritually starving world.

Practice your prayers over and over again, rather as you would if you had the leading part in a play. Many people object to this as they say that it feels as if they are acting it out rather than expressing a deep part of themselves. At first you will indeed be acting it out; you will be experimenting with the prayer and learning where to put the emphasis to invoke the greatest feeling. Eventually, the prayer will become a part of you and will live inside you and express your deepest feeling. Start in the same way as an actor does. Learn the lines, feel the inner meaning of the words, and then say the words with the full physical, mental and spiritual projection of which you are capable.

An experienced and effective dynamic pray-er can be equated to an experienced and effective actor. Imagine the wonderful Shakespearian actors who have studied their lines for so long that they live within them. They understand all the nuances of feeling that Shakespeare intended for the part, and through hours of practice they can evoke that feeling in themselves and in their audience. When you hear such actors you no longer think of them as actors, as they are really living the part they are playing. As with the actors, you will be acting at first, especially if you are not used to praying out loud, but eventually the prayers will become a pure expression of your soul.

5. Detachment

Another secret of success with our prayers is to give them everything we have and then detach from the results. Performing the mudra (hand sign) of detachment at the end of our spiritual practices helps us detach.

Place the palm of your right hand over the palm of your left hand in a sweeping motion. (See Figure 9.) This closes the psychic centers that are radiating spiritual energy in the palms of your hands. Also, it symbolically represents your detachment from the results of your prayer or healing. By performing the mudra of detachment you are saying, "I have done my work, now I leave it in the hands of the Creator to do the rest." Once you have sent healing to a person, you have done all you can and it is pointless to keep worrying about him or her. The secret of success in all spiritual practices is to work as hard as you can at them, and then detach.

If you follow the above practice of dynamic prayer, in full faith, you can perform virtual miracles on Earth. Prayer expresses the divinity within us all. As Dr. King wrote:

> *You carry a little miracle kit around with you; it's in your head, it's in your heart and if you have the right thought in your heart, and you control the thought in your head by the thought in your heart (the thought in your heart is called LOVE), you control that in the right way and direct it in the right way, you too can perform miracles.*

Step Seven Exercises
Prayer, the Song of the Soul

Day One: Stand in front of your altar with your hands raised in the prayer position. Practice the prayer on page 116 (or the one on page 118). Write it out and read it several times, then say it aloud. Then add as much feeling and love as you can.

Day Two: Once again say the prayer. This time say it as dynamically as you possibly can. It does not have to be loud enough to wake the neighbors, but make it urgent, dynamic and intense. Say it as if your life depended on it, remembering that someone's life might indeed depend upon your prayers. Make a point to learn this prayer.

Day Three: Say the prayer once again, dynamically. Then repeat it with all the reverence that you can. This time make it a gentle, humble and reverent expression of your innermost feeling. Fill your words with love and heart.

Day Four: Think of the prayer with love, and this time say it with every ounce of your concentration in the faith and knowledge that the results will come just as you say they will. Remember that action and reaction are opposite and equal. When you ask for a certain result, that result will come. That is why it is essential to be aware of your thoughts and desires and to keep them as noble as you can.

Day Five: Now write and construct your own prayer using as much love and thoughtfulness as you can. Learn your prayer by heart.

Day Six: Stand in front of your altar in the prayer position and say your prayer out loud with love, determination, respect and faith. It will be hard at first to insert all these ingredients into your prayer, but it will come in time. At first just imagine that a life depends on the prayer and give it your all.

Day Seven: Say both prayers, one after the other, and notice any effects you may feel. Write down how the prayers make you feel, emotionally and physically in your spiritual journal. You are now a spiritual energy radiator!

Step Eight
Healing, Nourishment for the Soul

Everyone can give spiritual healing in one degree or another. All you have to remember is between you and the Sun is 90 million miles of space full of energy that the Yogis call Prana or the Universal Life Forces, an essential part of which must be Love. All you have to do is remember that and send it out through your hands to a patient and it is as easy as that. It's all part of a Divine Plan and each and every person in the whole world and the whole of Creation is a part of that great Divine Plan...
—George King

The secret of health for both mind and body is not to mourn for the past, not to worry about the future, or to anticipate troubles, but to live the present moment wisely and earnestly.
—The Lord Buddha

This final step will teach you how to send spiritual healing to anyone who needs it. Healing, like prayer, is a vitally important part of this workout, because the soul expresses itself in an outpouring of the spiritual energy we call "Love." Sending healing to a person you never met, and may not even like, is one of the highest aspects of love or compassion to which we can aspire. When we are capable of a higher aspect of love than purely personal love, we feel for the trials and suffering of mankind and want to help. It is at this point that we can begin to obtain our highest spiritual growth.

Healing is one of the highest expressions of our soul. Healing knows no prejudice or boundaries; it knows no barriers of race, color or creed, no barriers of time or distance. We can heal our families in the same room, just as easily as we can heal a stranger across the world. The keys to healing are simply our desire to do so and an effective, safe technique.

By diligently practicing breathing exercises, affirmations, visualizations and prayers over the previous weeks, you are now better equipped to perform the important work of service to others. This is what our soul craves: to live a noble and compassionate life that reaches far beyond ourselves, outwards to mankind as a whole.

The Way of Enlightenment Today

The yogis and sages of the past gained enlightenment away from the crowds in remote caves in the Himalayas. Now enlightenment can be attained by the so-called ordinary person amidst the hustle and bustle of everyday life. This is because the need for spiritual, selfless action — or service to others — is now more urgent than ever before, as we enter the crucial and difficult transition from one astrological age to another. One of the simplest and most effective ways to give service is by sending absent healing — or healing over a distance. In this way because our motive is to help others, we will automatically advance ourselves through karma, the law of action and reaction.

It is now widely known that much of our sickness is psychosomatic, caused by stress, anxiety and negative thought patterns. Western medicine believes that the cause of disease is bacteria and germs, and that we have to remove them to have good health; healers regard things differently. The healer sees the bacteria and germs as an effect of the stress, anxiety and negative patterns. These latter psychological states affect the aura, cause blockages in the psychic centers, and may eventually break down the immune system, resulting in disease or imbalance.

Disease often starts in the aura of the person, the subtle egg-shaped envelope that encases our physical body. Our wrong thought and action causes blockages in the aura and psychic centers, which in turn reflect back onto the physical body as ill health. Through a method called Kirlian photography, actual photographs have been taken of the aura. It has been shown through these Kirlian photographs that disease appears in our subtle or energy bodies before it manifests in the physical.

When we are channels for healing power, that power flows through us into the aura and psychic centers of the person we are healing. This pure, vibrant energy of Love brings balance and harmony to the patient and in turn reflects onto his or her physical body so that better health results.

The Interrelationship of Life

Healing teaches that we are all interrelated. Once we understand this, we also realize that we can do no harm to anyone else without harming ourselves. The next logical step is to realize that we should not only do no harm but that we should consciously do the opposite — good. One way to "do good" is to radiate love. However, we are conditioned to think that love is a feeling and an emotion rather than energy. Love is not just something we fall into, it is energy that we can use to improve lives, an energy that has different qualities or levels of manifestation.

Service — Love in Action

The thought of love as an impersonal energy goes against the grain of our constant conditioning by television, films and magazines. We are led to believe that true love is warm and fuzzy and personal, but the great spiritual teachers who have moved our civilization forward have all had an all-encompassing, impersonal love for humanity. This is a far higher aspect of the same energy and is the mark of true greatness. We have to start somewhere and our healing and prayers will put us firmly on this path — the path to greatness.

We may feel inadequate, we may feel less than confident. We may feel we really cannot make a difference, but the truth is that everything we do makes a difference anyway. If we undertake our Workout for the Soul and all our everyday activities with love, then we will start to receive proof of love's power and efficacy. We will start to see the fruits of our labors of love.

The following true story is a wonderful illustration of the difference that love in action can make.

There was a quiet forest dweller who lived high above an Austrian village along the eastern slopes of the Alps. The old gentleman had been hired many years earlier by a young town councilman to clear away debris from the pools of water up in the mountain crevices that fed the lovely spring flowing through their town. With faithful, silent regularity, he patrolled the hills, removed the leaves and branches, and wiped away the silt that would otherwise have choked and contaminated the fresh flow of water. The village soon became a popular attraction for vacationers. Graceful swans floated along the crystal clear spring, the mill wheels of various businesses located near the water turned day and night, farmlands were naturally irrigated, and the view from restaurants was picturesque beyond description.

Years passed. One evening, the town council met for its semiannual meeting. As they reviewed the budget, one man's eye caught the salary figure being paid the obscure "keeper of the spring." The keeper of the purse asked, "Who is this old man? Why do we keep him on year after year? No one ever sees him. For all we know, the strange ranger of the hills is doing us no good. He isn't necessary any longer." By a unanimous vote, they dispensed with the old man's services.

For several weeks, nothing changed.

By early autumn, the trees began to shed their leaves. Small branches snapped off and fell into the pools, hindering the rushing flow of sparkling water. One afternoon, someone noticed a slight yellowish-brown tint in the spring. A few days later, the water was much darker. Within another week, a slimy film covered sections of the water along the banks, and a foul odor was soon detected. The mill wheels moved more slowly, some finally ground to a halt. Swans left, as did the tourists. Clammy fingers of disease and sickness reached deeply into the village.

Quickly, the embarrassed council called a special meeting. Realizing their gross error in judgment, they rehired the old keeper of the spring, and within a few weeks, the veritable river of life began to clear up. The wheels started to turn, and new life returned to the hamlet in the Alps.

Never become discouraged with the seeming smallness of your task, job, or life. Cling fast to the words of Edward Everett Hale:

I am only one, but still I am one. I cannot do everything, but still I can do something; and because I cannot do everything, I will not refuse to do something I can do.

Develop a Healing Consciousness

We are all an essential part of the whole, and all our thoughts and actions have a ripple effect that affects the whole. Once we realize this and really accept it into our lives, our outlook and way of thinking changes. We develop a "healing consciousness," where we bring harmony and light into the world through our conscientious actions and noble motivations. In this state, we do not seek glory or reward, but act in a way that our soul dictates we should. In time, this manifests not just as a prick of conscience, but as high intuition that will not be ignored. My own master summed it up in this aphorism: *If we take one step to God, It will take two steps towards us.*

You may already have a "healing consciousness" and not even be aware of it. When you see a child who is obviously sick or injured in some way, do you want to reach out and touch that child, to bring the child joy and laughter again? When you see a dog lurch out into traffic, does not your heart lurch with it? When an elderly person hesitates to cross the road, as traffic races past, do you want to rush over and help? You may say, of course, that is normal human kindness. Yes, it is and that is the wonderful quality which if expressed — and expression is the key, not just desire — can change our world.

Never underestimate kindness, which is one of the highest and noblest of qualities. Instead, kindness should be recognized and nurtured as a potent aspect of our soul's qualities. If we act from a viewpoint of kindness, we will not go far wrong. This is not weakness, which takes the line of least resistance, but strength. Jesus was so kind — compassionate beyond our comprehension — that he died a terrible death on our behalf, yet he was also so strong and powerful that he turned over the heavy, wooden tables of the moneylenders in the temple without hesitation. He was so brave that he faced the most evil among us, with his weapon always love in its highest aspect. Other great masters and avatars throughout history have suffered terribly so that they could help mankind as a whole.

Kindness is compassion that every day of our lives we are presented with opportunities to express. You will succeed many times, and sometimes you will fail, but the main thing is that you keep trying. Your kind acts embrace others and make them feel special, but they make you feel special, too. Kindness is the opposite of a vicious circle; it spirals upwards and is uplifting and generous in nature.

The first exercise in Step Eight is to perform conscious acts of kindness. Instead of just thinking about doing kind and thoughtful things, do them. Go out of your way to be kind. Then, make a note of all the opportunities that presented themselves to you and how you felt afterwards.

By developing a "healing consciousness," you then take this normal human quality of kindness a step further. Instead of just wanting to help the sick child, you reach out your hands to heal that child. Or if you cannot do that, you reach out with your mind's eye to send a beam of brilliant white healing light to the sick child in the faith that your love will make a difference. By doing this, you gain control over your wishes and make them a reality. Then you begin to gain great personal power, strength and confidence that you really can help to change the world. Miracles are within your grasp.

> The next time you see an ambulance rushing past with its lights flashing, no longer just feel sorry for the sick person inside. This time, act immediately by sending a mental beam of white healing light to the ambulance and the person inside, filling them with light and power. The more you do this, the better will be the results. You have to remember that every little bit helps — think always of the keeper of the spring. The person inside the ambulance could be hovering between life and death. This extra burst of energy might be exactly what he or she needs to keep on living.

Healing does not cure a person, but the healing energy enables that person to heal themselves. When people are sick they lack energy, they are weak, their psychic centers are not functioning properly and are blocked to some degree. Spiritual energy can remedy this through its wonderful healing, balancing power.

The Power of Healing

Unfortunately, spiritual energy cannot be measured at the moment, as our scientific instrumentation is still too coarse. However, it is similar to electricity and I predict that someday we will have sensitive equipment to measure it. There is no doubt that spiritual energy exists. When you have been healing for a long time, or if you are a powerful healer, you may feel spiritual energy as heat or cold, or as a tingling sensation in the palms of your hands or Heart Center. If you have received healing, you may feel it as a powerful sensation in your body.

However, the important thing is not so much how it feels, but the effect it has. In this way, it resembles electricity. We do not want to feel electricity because we know it will give us a shock. What we care about are its results! By the same token, you should not worry if you do not feel the power of spiritual energy at first. It is the results of spiritual energy that count.

I have been healing for over twenty years, and when I give healing I sometimes feel an opening of my Heart Center and increased mental pressure. I also feel changes occurring in the patient's physical body and aura. Often I feel heat or a tingling sensation in my hands, which is quite common. I know the energy is flowing and many of my patients have remarked that they feel the healing power. Also, I have had many excellent results over the years, including the instantaneous healing of a broken foot, and many instant headache and migraine cures. Because many healers feel strong physical sensations such as these, you should monitor anything you feel when you send your healing over a distance.

When you receive healing, you are in a receptive state and may feel the healing very strongly, generally as heat in the body. However, the energy can also be cool, especially if you are suffering from a heated condition such as a fever. The wonderful thing about healing energy is that the body of the patient will extract from this power the exact frequency that it needs for the healing to take place. When you send out white healing light, the best color to use at this stage, the subconscious mind of the patient will extract the color frequency it needs for the healing to take place. For example, if the patient has a fever, the energy extracted will be from the cooling blue end of the spectrum,.

In your healing work, keep in mind that while every disease condition can be healed, you will not necessarily be able to cure every patient. A person's health is subject to the great law of karma, just like everything else in Creation. It may be the right time for a person to get better, or the soul of that person may dictate that he or she still has more to learn from that particular illness. However, it is not up to us to judge; we should always try to help. Healing will always be beneficial in one way or another.

Burning Desire

With healing, the place to start is in your own mind. You should not worry about what you feel, or what you think you should be feeling. Like anything else, the desire to heal can also be learned. On the path to inner fitness, you should not worry about whether or not you are in the mood to do something. There will probably be times when you do not feel like doing your spiritual practices, giving healing to someone or doing anything else that takes effort.

I have heard people warn that you should never undertake spiritual work of any kind unless you are in the right mood to do it. However, I say that if you always wait for the right mood, you will probably not do it very often. As part of the journey towards the expression of the soul, you can learn to control your moods and feelings. The Workout for the Soul will help you accomplish this.

I have often thought to myself, "I really don't feel like sending any healing today," but then I go ahead and send it anyway. Afterwards, I feel good because "I," the higher part of me, not my fickle, conscious mind, has gained control. There have also been times when I have failed. I am sure you will experience all these things, but the main thing is that step by step, you are making progress. Eventually these spiritual tools will feel as natural to you as cleaning your teeth.

We all have to face our "dark nights of the soul." There will probably be times when you do not even care about your own advancement, let alone the fate of mankind. At these times, go to your sacred space and spend a few minutes thinking deeply about suffering in some form. Force yourself to do it, even if you do not want to do it. Feel yourself moved to tears almost, and then you will find that you have re-established a link to the deeper part of your nature. It will be far easier for you to then raise your hands in healing. Once you have done this, you will almost always feel better. You may well find that your original bleak mood has lifted.

Few of us are saints. My Master was the most spiritual person I could ever dream of meeting and I was blessed to spend many years studying and working with him. Dr. King spent his entire adult life in complete surrender to God and in service to mankind. He used every ounce of his compassion and genius towards that end and left behind a spiritual legacy that will benefit mankind for generations to come. Despite that, even he never regarded himself as a saint or a holy person, though many begged to differ.

You do not have to worry about everything you think or say, but the more you adjust to a richer, deeper spiritual life, the easier it will be to make changes, the more frequently you will have that burning desire to really help others, and the more real fulfillment you will feel.

Healing Over a Distance

Absent Healing, one of the fastest and most effective ways to change for the better, is an extension of the visualization exercises you practiced earlier. If you do it often enough you will develop the "healing consciousness" mentioned earlier. Absent Healing resembles hands-on healing, which is also known as pranic healing, energy healing, faith healing or spiritual healing. Whichever technique you learn, the principle behind it is the sending of healing energy from point A, the healer, to point B, the patient, to bring about a state of balance within the patient.

When my Master first taught this, people thought he oversimplified the facts, yet this is exactly how healing works. He also taught that healing was the birthright of everyone on earth, dispelling the myth that healing is a special gift reserved for the few. Now the latter truth is more generally accepted, but twenty years ago it was not. His approach to healing was not only ahead of its time, but also extremely simple. As only the best teacher can, he had the genius to cut through all the layers of complexity and find the simplicity. Unfortunately, our conscious minds tend to try and convince us that the more difficult a thing sounds, the more profound it must be.

Healing is not only very simple, but a natural ability of us all. We were born to heal and you may already have had the experience of reaching out to touch a person who is sick or injured in some way. It is a natural instinct and natural way of life to want to channel love energy from the strong to the weak. Through healing, you are slowly but surely returning to the great natural laws of Creation.

Absent Healing represents an extension of this urge to reach out and touch. When we hear that someone we love on the other side of the world is sick and suffering, we feel a natural urge to want to help, to reach out and touch that person. Through Absent Healing, you can do just that. You can touch others, not just physically with your hands, but even more profoundly with your love. Through using this Absent Healing technique you can send the higher aspects of love out across the ethers of space to another soul anywhere in the world.

As I have said before, we are all virtual radiators of spiritual energy. Why else would we have the higher psychic centers that we have? If we were just here to live, breathe, eat, mate, be successful in business and make money, we would not need the higher psychic centers. Although these are closed or dysfunctional in many people, our purpose is to open them fully and consciously and so become the noble, compassionate, wise souls that we really are. Through healing and prayer you will start to open and activate the higher psychic centers, progressing firmly on the spiritual path.

Absent Healing Technique

So far in this step we have practiced acts of kindness and are learning to develop a healing consciousness. Now we are actually going to send healing over a distance. This will be a part of the fifteen-minute Workout for the Soul.

> 1. To prepare for the absent healing service, you should purchase another notebook apart from your spiritual journal to use as an absent healing book. In this notebook, write down the names of people who need healing. These may be friends and family, or strangers that you have heard about on the news. It doesn't matter who they are or where they are geographically, you just need to have their names. We are all linked to

each other by invisible "etheric" links; the vibration of what and who we are constantly radiates outwards through the ethers through the name we use.

2. You may also want to construct a healing prayer that you can learn and use in your healing service. Write this down in your book and learn it by heart. The more you learn and use it, the more it will start to live within you and the more power the prayer will have. You can construct your new prayer using the formula given in Step Seven, or you may wish to use the following healing prayer:

> *Oh divine and wondrous Creator*
> *I pray that your healing power may flow through me now*
> *In a stream of love and light*
> *To those who will be named.*
> *I pray that these ones may be strengthened and inspired*
> *Protected and healed at this time.*
> *I thank Thee, Oh Wondrous One*
> *For this opportunity to be of service*
> *And pray that Thy Divine Will may be done.*

3. Once again, sit in front of your altar and practice the Complete Breath, with the palms of your hands facing down on your knees. Be very calm and still, and ensure that you are relaxed around your neck and shoulders. Remember that tension restricts the flow of spiritual energy through you. Keep your spine straight with your head in line with your spine and your feet flat on the floor.

4. Raise your hands up, with your palms facing outwards in the prayer position as described in Step Seven, and with as much feeling and love as you can, say aloud your healing prayer. By saying this prayer aloud, you will start to activate the healing power.

5. Now visualize a pure, vibrant white light radiating from your Heart Center, in front of your breastbone, and from the palms of your hands. Really try and visualize this light until you feel it flowing through you. Some people feel it is a tingling sensation

in their hands, but do not worry about the feeling. Just concentrate on sending it out. Do not even worry if you cannot visualize it as a white light. This may take time and practice. All you need to do is to keep visualizing that you are sending out healing power. You will definitely be radiating out spiritual healing power, even though initially you may not feel or see it.

6. Read aloud the name of the first person on your list. The spiritual energy will then flow to that person to bring about balance within that person's aura, which will reflect back into their physical body, bringing balance, harmony and ease. Whatever you do, do not visualize a sick person. Even if you know the person is seriously ill, do not visualize them as such. Instead, visualize just the white light leaving you and flowing out to them. If you have the time during your healing service, and you know the person you are sending healing to, you can visualize that person being absolutely filled with pure vibrant white light.

7. Let the power continue to flow through you, your hands and your Heart Center for a minute or two. Imagine it as a stream of energy. Realize that this healing power is an aspect of true Love. Try and feel the love and compassion filling you and flowing through you.

8. Read aloud the second name from your list and again continue sending out love for a few seconds before reading out the next name.

9. When you have finished, close your service with another simple prayer. In this prayer, thank the Creator for the opportunity you have had to be a channel for healing power. Also request that, if it be the Creator's will, these people be healed. It is important to state your intent in your prayers, as discussed earlier.

10. Close by swiping your right hand over your left hand once, using the mudra of detachment.

You are now a healer and can claim this as your birthright!

Step Eight Exercises
Healing: Nourishment for the Soul

Day One: Sit quietly in front of your altar with hands palms-down on your knees and spine straight. Be relaxed. Go within and think about your part in the whole. Think of yourself as an integral part of your family; then of your community; then your country; finally, visualize yourself in the world. See yourself as a radiant, positive being and then imagine yourself as such in your family group; then in your community; then in your country; and finally in the world. Realize that this can be true. It is up to you.

Day Two: Perform the same visualization again. Spend the day seeking opportunities for acts of kindness and write these down at the end of the day.

Day Three: Develop a healing consciousness. Mentally radiate a vibrant, white light. Next time you are outside and you see an ambulance pass with its lights flashing, send out this brilliant white light as a beam of healing power to the person in the ambulance. This will only take a second or two, but the more you practice, the better it will be. Your mental healing could prove the difference between life and death; you will never know. Do the same thing when you next see a sick person, a dying tree or plant. Practice this whenever you can until it becomes an extension of you.

Day Four: Sit silently in front of your altar and once again go within. Determine that you will develop the desire to give healing. Do this by concentrating upon the suffering of others, or by feeling inspired by others you know who have made a difference to the world through their spiritual efforts.

Day Five: Practice the Absent Healing technique (page 139).

Day Six: Practice the Absent Healing technique.

Day Seven: Recall any results or feelings you had during the week and write these down in your spiritual journal.

Putting It All Together
in 15 Minutes a Day

Following the light of the sun, we left the Old World.
—Inscription on Columbus' caravels

Destiny is not a matter of chance, it is a matter of choice; it is not a thing to be waited for, it is a thing to be achieved.
—William Jennings Bryan

After following the previous eight steps in this book, you are now fully prepared to begin your 15-minute Workout for the Soul. Enlightenment dawns in stages. Slowly and gradually we learn through experience, through our spiritual studies, through self-analysis, self-mastery and service to others. The journey within is the shortest in distance, but takes longer to complete than any other. This spiritual workout speeds you on this journey and protects and guides you every step along the way.

The world abounds with spiritual theory, but what we really need is spiritual action. Only spiritual action really changes us and helps change our world for the better. Enjoy this Workout for the Soul and begin to manifest the infinite riches and power of the divine spark within you.

15-Minute Workout for the Soul

Aim to do this workout a minimum of three and a maximum of seven days every week.

The workout consists of eight steps, with approximate timings for each step, making a total of fifteen minutes. This serves only as an initial guideline for you that you can adapt as you go along. At first, I would advise you to read the instructions as you do it, until you are completely confident that you are practicing the whole workout correctly. You should refer to the previous steps in this book as often as you need to, so that you clearly understand the purpose, benefits and effects of this Workout for the Soul.

Perform this workout as perfectly as you can until you feel as if it lives within you. At that point, continue practicing for an additional few weeks and note down any experiences or changes you may feel. You may feel inspired to add an extra prayer, to do more breathing exercises, or more healing. That is fine, but ensure that you develop slowly and carefully, just as you would with any other discipline in your life.

Step One: Preparing the Temple (one minute)

Be seated in front of your altar. (See Figure 12.) Remove any metal from your body, especially your hands and fingers. Place your hands palms-downward on your thighs, with your middle fingers

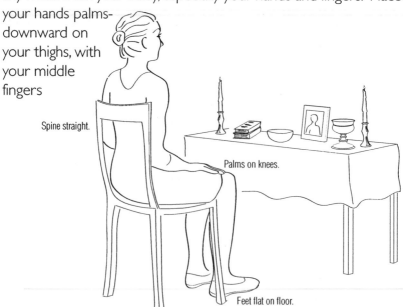

Spine straight.

Palms on knees.

Feet flat on floor.

Figure 12.
Person Seated Before Altar

approximately two inches above the knees, at the point where there is a minor psychic center. You may feel this point as a slight depression or sensitive spot in your legs.

Relax your neck and shoulders and feel comfortable in your seat with feet flat on the floor and your spine straight, head in line with your spine. Now close your eyes, detach from your environment and go within.

Step Two: Refreshing the Soul (one minute)

Be thankful for this opportunity to reach within and feel appreciation for all the rich experiences of your life. Allow this attitude of mind to bring you calm and inner peace.

Step Three: Harmonizing with the Breath of Life (two minutes)

Be very still and concentrate on your breathing. Breathe very deeply and evenly and practice the Complete Breath. Take a deep breath in and relax your abdomen as your diaphragm descends; then allow your rib cage to expand outwards and upwards. Finally use the upper portion of your lungs. Hold your breath for a second and exhale slowly. At the end, your abdomen should be slightly drawn in. This is done in one continuous movement with each phase of the breathing merging with the next, like the swell of the ocean.

Step Four: Awakening Your Creative Powers (one minute)

Allow your thoughts to float before your mind and then just watch them until you start to gain control of them. Do not be attached to your thoughts. You are detaching from all your cares and worries, and all that has gone before you. You are existing in the Now, in the present moment, in peace.

Step Five: Visualizing Mystic Practices (two minutes)

Now using your powers of visualization, practice the White Light and the Violet Flame. (See Figure 7., page 90) In your mind's eye, see a brilliant beam of white light coming down through space. See and feel it entering your brain, purifying every cell of your brain as it does so. Bring this pure white light down through your head and shoulders and into your Heart Center. See and feel this brilliant light entering and filling your Heart Center.

Now think downwards to Mother Earth and be aware of this great planetary home beneath your feet. Make a reverent request to this great Mother, for her beautiful Violet Flame of protection and transmutation. See and feel this coming up from the Logos of earth, through your feet and legs. Take it right up through your body and aura, out through the top of your head, to a distance of 20 or 30 feet above your head.   Hold this visualization for about 20 seconds.

Step Six: Building a Bridge to Your Soul (one minute)

Remember that one of the most direct ways to manifest your higher self is through the use of positive, spiritual affirmation. By repeating the affirmation, "I am the Divine Presence which is creating perfection throughout my whole life," you are programming your subconscious mind correctly; you are affirming to yourself the truth that within you are the infinite powers and riches of Divinity itself. Repeat this to yourself silently but with concentration and intensity for about thirty seconds.

Step Seven: Prayer, the Song of the Soul (two minutes)

Offer a prayer of thankfulness and guidance. You can either write one yourself, or use the following. Remember to raise your hands in the prayer mudra with the palms facing outwards as you do so. First visualize the prayer energy radiating out as a pure, white light. Then just allow it to flow as you say the prayer with all your feeling and love.

Oh Divine One
I thank you for this opportunity to go within
And contact Thy Mighty Light.
I pray for Thy strength, guidance, healing and protection
To fill and surround me at this time;
And I pray that I may become an instrument for Thy Work
So that I may be of greater service to our world.
Oh Mighty One
May Thy Divine Will be done.

After saying this prayer, remain silent for a minute and allow the spiritual energy to flow through you, filling and surrounding you, like a great river of light and love coursing through you.

Step Eight: Healing, Nourishment for the Soul (three minutes)

This is the absent healing section of your workout, which will strengthen you spiritually, as well as help others.

Keep your hands raised in the prayer mudra and say the following prayer with all your love, concentration, intensity, feeling and belief:

> *Oh divine and wondrous God*
> *I pray that Thy healing power may flow through me at this moment;*
> *To the following people*
> *So that they may be strengthened and inspired*
> *So that, if it be Thy Will oh God*
> *They may be healed at this time.*

Now read aloud the names of people who are sick and need healing. You may want to keep a list of names that you read on your Altar. Do not be afraid to let the people know you are sending them healing. If you know the people you are sending healing to, visualize them being filled with this pure light, but do not visualize their illness.

Also, if you know of a natural disaster or some kind of tragedy that has taken place, you should send out your prayers to the victims and their families and to the relief workers to give them strength. Continue silently sending out healing power for as long as you wish, visualizing a white light flowing outwards from you as a stream of pure healing light.

Once you feel that the power has flowed, just end the healing with a little prayer, such as the following:

> *I thank Thee, Oh Wondrous God*
> *For listening to my prayer*
> *And thank you for this opportunity to be of service.*
> *I pray that, if it be Thy will*
> *They may be healed at this time.*

Completion: The Practice of the Presence (two minutes)

Now end with the mystical visualization of the Practice of the Presence. (See diagrams 8a, 8b and 8c, pages 91-93.)

Place your left hand over your Solar Plexus Center and your right hand on top of the left. Once again, use your powers of visualization to imagine and bring into being a pure, white scintillating light. See this coming down into your brain and feel it charging every cell of your brain. Take it through your shoulders and into your Heart Center.

Now visualize the Violet Flame coursing up through you from the heart of the great Goddess beneath your feet, cleansing, uplifting, purifying. See this coming up and take it into the Heart Center.

In your mind's eye, join together the white light and the violet flame in the Heart Center and take these two forces as one up through your spine at the back and out through the top of your head. Now visualize a beautiful golden sphere above the top of your head. Know that this is the Divine Spark of God within us all. See this wonderful golden orb suspended there, like a miniature Sun. In great reverence, offer into this golden sphere the White Light and the Violet Flame.

Now bring down from this sphere its wonderful golden essence of complete Spirituality. See and feel it coursing through not only your physical body, but also your subtle bodies, filling you with its golden Light of God Itself. Know that this Divine Essence is bringing you the wisdom, strength, love and understanding that you need in your journey through experience, back to God.

Now, say out loud the affirmation: *Great Peace, Great Peace, Great Peace. Thy Divine Will Oh Mighty God be Done.*

Then use the Mudra of Detachment. Just sweep the right-hand palm over the left-hand palm once. This has the effect of cutting off the flow of spiritual energy from your palm centers, symbolically allowing you to detach from this workout and move onto another activity in your daily routine.

Your workout is now complete and you should get into the habit of writing down any experiences and impressions in your spiritual journal so that you can monitor your progress.

This is a short but extremely powerful workout. The more you do it, the more inner fitness you will attain. After performing this for several months, the next step is for you to introduce more advanced breathing, concentration and contemplation exercises, as well as further practice of other mystic prayer practices to increase your spiritual energy radiation. You may also wish to introduce the repetition of holy mantra into your workout. In the following section, "Enhancing Your Workout," I explain the ways in which you can do this.

At times you will be faced with difficult choices. Pause before making your choices and contact the source within you by going into the silence of your sacred space. Then practice your Workout for the Soul, gather your inner strength and afterwards remain seated in a reflective state until you feel calm, peaceful and detached from your problems. Then you will be ready to make your decisions in a balanced fashion, with your head as well as your heart.

Always remember that everyone faces challenges and tests in their lives. Recognize these tests as opportunities for your soul to speak through you and provide you with the answers. All you have to do is to learn how to listen and remain open and receptive to the answers. Eventually you will receive the guidance you need.

The choice we all face is whether we should live our life on the surface or whether we should courageously reach deeper into the richness, mystery, beauty and power of the soul within. Remember, all that glitters is not gold, even though it may appear to be. Everything spiritual is more precious than the most precious metal and far more lasting.

Thank you for joining me on this journey to inner strength and fitness. It has been my pleasure to help you to achieve these spiritual goals. May you continue to grow in love, confidence, joy and faith and go onwards and upwards along your journey to manifesting your limitless soul potential and to self-mastery. May this spiritual workout gradually spread its power and influence throughout all your days, weeks and years to come. May God be with you to guide and inspire you always.

Enhancing Your Workout

The universe is full of magical things,
patiently waiting for our wits to grow sharper.
—Eden Phillpotts

The true meaning of life is to plant trees,
under whose shade you do not expect to sit.
—Nelson Henderson

This step is for those of you who have been practicing the Workout for the Soul for a while and now wish to make this workout even more powerful and effective. You can do this by introducing more advanced practices that extend and enhance the workout.

Further Advanced Practices

If you are really serious about your advancement and soul work, the two most powerful things you can introduce into this workout are advanced pranayama (breathing exercises) and mantra yoga. There are numerous yoga books giving advanced breathing exercises and I would certainly recommend you study these. However, if you want to find a powerful system that will enhance this workout and will only add another ten or fifteen minutes to your practice, I would highly recommend the breathing exercises given by my Master, Dr. George King. He devised this brilliant sequence after years of intensive and advanced yoga training, and it also includes affirmations and visualizations. This sequence is available in the last publication written by Dr. King, together with fellow author and close student, Dr. Richard Lawrence. The publication is entitled, *Realize Your Inner Potential.* and offers an ideal complement to the present book.

As far as mantra is concerned, again I would recommend the above publication. In it Dr. King — who was a Master of Mantra Yoga — gives several of these that you can use in your workout. When mantra is chanted, it builds spiritual power and enhances the vibrations of the practitioner as well as his or her surroundings. As such, you should use mantra prior to performing the prayer and healing parts of the workout, in order to "charge" yourself in readiness for sending out spiritual energy.

Radiation of Spiritual Energy

You can improve this important aspect in many different ways. In the East they have many methods to develop prana or chi and increase your capacity for power radiation. Chi, or prana, is the universal life force that permeates all creation. It powers the greatest Sun through space and yet causes our own hearts to beat and our blood to flow. Without it we would be lifeless. When we have it in abundance and in balance, we have tremendous energy, a radiant vitality for life and a strong, healthy body and mind. Chi Kung is the science of developing and controlling chi. Until recently, it was a closely guarded secret for thousands of years. Now you can find many books and excellent teachers in this ancient way of health and spiritual advancement.

The many different forms of yoga are all designed to aid in your enlightenment. Hatha Yoga, which concentrates on physical postures, and Kundalini Yoga both enhance the flow of prana in the body and your power radiation ability. You will find many books and classes on Hatha Yoga, but attempt Kundalini Yoga only under an experienced and proven teacher, as it can be dangerous if not performed correctly.

You can also attend the intensive workshops and classes on personal development conducted in different parts of the world by The Aetherius Society where experienced instructors will give you individual attention.

Powerful Prayers

Another way to enhance your workout involves the use of powerful prayers designed to radiate spiritual power. I could not write about prayer without mentioning a book of prayers and teachings called *The Twelve Blessings*. These sacred texts were delivered through the advanced mediumship abilities of my spiritual master, Dr. George King, by no less a Personage than Jesus Himself. They were delivered in England, in 1958, on twelve consecutive Sundays.

At the time, my Master did not know who would be speaking through him, so the first of The Twelve Blessings was introduced by a prominent member of the Spiritual Hierarchy of Earth, known as Saint Goo-Ling. Then the wonderful voice of the great Avatar of Love came through Dr. King as he sat in a highly elevated yogic trance condition, known in the east as *Samadhi*. The thought impulses of the great Master Jesus were sent to Dr. King and translated into sound using his larynx. The result was a series of profound, mystical, inspiring teachings for the New Age. They are an extension of The Sermon on the Mount, including a Cosmic Concept.

By reading this book by Dr. King, one can learn much from the deeply mystical texts. By practicing the prayers and blessings contained within his book, one can send out streams of spiritual light to our world. The book was delivered so that it can be used by anyone to help ease us into the New Age of Peace and Enlightenment in a gentler manner than our present karmic pattern deserves. It offers another great manipulation from the great Avatar, Jesus, on behalf of all mankind.

Everyone I know who has studied and practiced The Twelve Blessings has been profoundly moved by it. Many people express that it has changed their lives and enhanced their whole awareness of the myriad aspects of Creation, of which we are a part. I highly recommend that you study and use this wonderful book to enhance your Workout for the Soul.

Karma

Every time you practice this Workout for the Soul you will also obtain "karmic benefits." Karma is the law of cause and effect: one of the great Laws of the Creator Itself. Everything you think and do has an opposite and equal reaction, which is also one of the basic laws of physics, as well as metaphysics. Although people talk about karma now, few really think deeply about this exact law, which governs Creation. If you do think deeply about it you will realize that you are responsible for every thought and action.

Each of us has what is called a "karmic pattern." This is the sum total of the results of all our previous thoughts and actions. Your individual and unique karmic pattern is made up of your actions, hopes, dreams and failures of the past. It determines the lessons you have to overcome in order to evolve. Your karmic pattern creates pressure in you to change.

We've all experienced being faced with decisions and choices, whether in a relationship, a job, or some other situation. Perhaps we took the easy way out and did not learn the lesson presented. As a result, this very same lesson will appear again further down the road, in a somewhat different guise. Perhaps we will fail to learn the lesson a second time. Then it appears repeatedly until we finally recognize it and gather our strength and experience to overcome it. Once we have learned one lesson, we can then go on to the next, through lives of experience, until we gain self-mastery or enlightenment.

The path to spiritual growth is long and tough but extremely rewarding. There is no getting around our karmic pattern, though we can delay it. However, by delaying the learning of lessons, we end up suffering as a result. The way out is to take definite spiritual action. This Workout for the Soul will assist you in recognizing your lessons as they come. It will also assist you in gaining strength and courage to face these lessons and the wisdom to face them correctly.

Because of this, you may feel that your life is speeding up, with many new challenges coming your way. However, when this starts to happen to you, you can rest assured that it is because you are making progress. At these times, intensify your workouts and draw upon your inner resources. Listen to the prompting of your soul and you will win. There is no promise that the spiritual path is an easy one, only that it is a fascinating and richly rewarding one.

Another aspect of karma is that while each of us has an individual karmic pattern, mankind also has a collective karmic pattern. Just as we are all helped in some degree by the great saints among us, so too are we pulled back by those who work for our downfall. Since we are linked together, by actively working toward spiritual growth, we are not only helping ourselves but also our families, friends and the whole world.

Spiritual actions are never wasted. People love to save money as their security. Some money is essential, but offers little true security; we can die at any moment or lose it all on the stock market. The results of every spiritual thought, action, prayer or healing pass are saved up for us in our "spiritual bank account." They accumulate and gather interest and you can never lose on them! In fact, when you die and are eventually reborn they will stand you in good stead. If your spiritual bank account is healthy, then you can look forward to an abundant future life full of opportunity and growth. This Workout for the Soul is one of the best investments you can make!

Service

Service to others has been mentioned throughout this book as the key to our advancement, as indeed it is. The more we help others, the greater we become from a soul point of view. We should no longer divorce ourselves from the world in order to find enlightenment, but work within the world to raise enlightenment through giving service.

There are many different ways to give service and if you are not already doing so, and wish to enhance your soul growth, I recommend that you select a way that feels right for you. There are many wonderful charities and volunteer organizations, such as Medicins sans Frontières, Children's Charities of America, and Red

Cross. The list is endless. We all can do something, no matter how small, to help a cause that touches our hearts and that benefits others less fortunate.

You can also give service through radiating spiritual energy. This Workout for the Soul enables you to help bring light, love and humanity to our world. Service is needed not only on the physical level, but also on the spiritual level. The biggest energy crisis today is the spiritual energy crisis — the lack of spiritual energy available. Prayer and healing help solve this.

Assistance from Higher Powers

This section is the most controversial, yet also the most important. However, no important advance in history ever occurred without being surrounded by controversy. The nature of mankind is that we do not like to change; we often resist change by striking out at anyone who presents us with the opportunity to change, despite the fact that it may benefit us. Those of you who are reading this book have already displayed courage; I ask you now to take another step forward, in faith and with an open mind. All I ask is that you accept that it may be true and then try and find out for yourself in a way that I will tell you later.

Many people believe, as I always have, that we are not alone in the universe. I think most people now accept this fact. Some also believe that we have been — and are being — visited by other more advanced races from other planets, some even within our solar system. At this point you may throw up your hands in horror. How can that be! We have sent spacecraft to several of the planets, where there is no evidence of life. Of course mankind always expects that life is exactly like we are, needing the conditions that we need to survive.

I believe that life exists on some of the other planets in a highly advanced spiritual form, similar to the form we take when we pass on and continue to exist on the subtle planes. Our track record on this earth is not too impressive and it has always seemed obvious to me that we are not the pinnacle of evolution as some people still seem to think.

I have studied the subject and am convinced that extraterrestrial visitors have been here and are here now to help us. My spiritual Master taught this also. In fact, this was one reason I studied with him for so many years — because everything he said was in keeping with my own previous beliefs and research, and yet he went much further. Apart from his mediumship of *The Twelve Blessings* he also received over six hundred messages from many other highly elevated and advanced beings from beyond this world.

One piece of information he received was that a giant spacecraft, invisible to radar, was visiting this planet for certain periods each year to help mankind. These spiritually advanced beings who have watched over us for centuries and who cooperate with The Great White Brotherhood of Earth, are also technologically far superior to us. Their spacecraft, called Satellite No. 3, has the task of enhancing all spiritual activities taking place anywhere on Earth at any time by an exact factor of three thousand times.

Since the fifties, for several periods each year this massive spacecraft has come into the orbit of our earth, 1550 miles above the surface. On board is a fantastic array of radionic instruments, manned by these spiritually evolved Masters. This advanced spacecraft is able to beam uplifting spiritual energy to anyone who is engaged in some type of spiritual act, whether directly helping another or working to improve themselves spiritually. It makes no difference what race or religion they may be. The energy goes to Christians, Hindus, Buddhists, Taoists, Jews, people of all religions, and even to atheists if they are working for the common good. During this period the karmic effects of each spiritual action are enhanced three thousand times, thereby speeding the evolution of both the individual and mankind as a whole.

Higher powers have always been there for us, despite mankind's disregard for them and they will be into the distant future.

Sounds incredible? Yes. Sounds impossible? Not really. I always used to imagine myself as an advanced being who could fly and visit other planets and come back here. When I returned in my imagination I would always feel very sad at the beauty of the planet contrasted by the ignorance of mankind as a whole.

As a young person I could not comprehend that we were actually killing each other, for from my position in space I just saw us as one race of people, all with the same hopes, fears, dreams and problems. All learning, all growing, all striving in different ways, all with good hearts, though some covered up through lives of hatred and suffering. What a sad time I had, until I managed to put on my superwoman's suit and beam down my love energy to all the suffering people and make them into the shining, joyful, beautiful beings they really were.

A childhood fantasy, maybe, but when I first heard of Satellite No. 3 it made so much sense to me. It seemed obvious that this was the very thing that a technologically and spiritually superior race of people would do. Not only that but I found that when I did my spiritual practices during the periods of time when Satellite No. 3 was in orbit I felt these practices were definitely enhanced.

Let me give you an example of the magic of Satellite No. 3. I am English and spent some years promoting spirituality in England. In the process, I was interviewed on many radio programs and had a regular weekly slot at a radio station near Brighton in the South of England, which took place in the late evening. One evening I decided to talk to the listeners about Satellite No. 3. I asked them all to stop what they were doing and raise their hands to send out spiritual energy through prayer, in cooperation with Satellite No. 3. It was an extremely powerful few minutes but as this was not a call-in program I did not have any feedback from the listeners at the time.

The interviewer felt quite bowled over by the power and expressed this over the airwaves. The next day he called me excitedly, telling me that there had been a tremendous response. People had been calling in saying they had had all sorts of wonderful experiences. They had seen light and felt love. They had felt uplifted and felt healing power flowing through them. One lady, who had not had the courage to leave her house for years, was able to go outside for the first time. Another gentleman was healed of a longstanding health problem. The calls continued all week and hit the front page of the local newspaper.

It is very difficult to receive proof of spiritual and metaphysical things, as they are beyond the physical realm with which science deals. However, this offered proof of another kind. Proof of the best kind — results! Unfortunately, as is too often the case in our world, the controversy that was aroused sparked the heavy hand of conservatism, so that the interviewer eventually lost his job. The program, which had been delightfully open-minded and broad, was closed down. Nevertheless, truth never goes away, despite mankind's limitations or ignorance.

The dates of the orbit of Satellite No. 3, referred to as Spiritual Pushes, were given through Dr. King as follows:

April 18 — May 23
July 5 — August 5
September 3 — October 9
November 4 — December 10

Satellite No. 3 enters and leaves Earth's orbit, at exactly 12:00 midnight Greenwich Mean Time. The entire period of each of these Spiritual Pushes is extremely potent for all spiritual practices and selfless actions. The first and last hours of the orbit of this Satellite are particularly powerful. You can experience this for yourself by tuning in and performing your spiritual practices at this time. (Note: Convert the above GMT time to your local time.)

I don't ask you to believe me, but try it for yourselves. Allow your minds to soar above the limitations of earth. Tune into this giant spacecraft and its wonderful source of spiritual energy, and you may be surprised at the difference this makes to your practices. We have been told that the energy used by Satellite No. 3 comes directly from the Sun. The Sun, as has been known to metaphysicians and Eastern Masters for centuries, is the source for all prana or spiritual energy on Earth. Satellite No. 3 magnifies this energy in a safe and highly effective manner and directs it to those working for the greater good on Earth.

Dr. George King — Western Master of Yoga

This book would not be complete without a more complete reference to my Master, Dr. George King. All of his many books and audiocassettes, many of which are cited in the bibliography, are designed to enhance you in your spiritual journey.

You may wonder why Dr. King was chosen for the monumental tasks I have mentioned. All I can say is that he had the necessary experience, qualifications and strength of character. He was an advanced master of yoga in his own right. Just to work with him was to be impressed by his focus and concentration of purpose, his relentless pursuit of his spiritual goals, genius and sheer hard work. All thoughts of time away from his main purpose in life were anathema. His was truly a life of service lived, in his own words, in "unconditional surrender to God."

In his twenties, he began to develop his already considerable abilities through the study of Yoga and the practice of various occult and healing sciences. This resulted in a series of personal initiations that he never spoke much about, but which were highly advanced and received from very exalted sources indeed. He also began to manifest great psychic and occult powers, such as healing, levitation, clairvoyance, invisibility and control of the forces of nature — the Devic Kingdom.

In 1954, Dr. King engaged upon a program of metaphysical research. He was renowned as a spiritual healer, medium and psychic, and was in communication with some of the great healers and scientists in the other realms, such as Sir James Young Simpson and Sir Oliver Lodge.

While the international metaphysical organization, The Aetherius Society, founded by Dr. King in England in 1955, achieved tremendous publicity throughout the years, his passing in 1997 was unnoticed by the world as a whole. There are many reasons for this. He had a job to do that was far more important than gaining public recognition. This was a global mission of service to humanity — and much more. He did not just feed mankind with the spiritual food of his wisdom and profound teachings, he also taught us how we can give spiritual food — in the form of healing and enlightenment — to our brothers and sisters throughout the world.

His experiences up to his passing and the advanced initiations he received had given him tremendous self-discipline, courage and reverence for the truth. He also had a dynamic determination, reinforced by tremendous mental and psychic powers. And he had a dogged persistence. For example, when he was contacted by the Master Jesus, in 1958, he received death threats from those who thought this work was blasphemous, and from those who were jealous of the implications. However, despite this he continued undeterred, as he did with all his work on behalf of mankind. He pushed forward the limits of science and spirituality and combined them both in global healing missions of great power and influence. For the time he was on earth, he illumined the mental realms of earth with his genius and enabled us to appreciate more deeply the wonders of the universe and creation and the mysteries of life.

Although not yet universally recognized, I predict that Dr. King will go down in history as one of the most fascinating spiritual teachers who attained the highest states of consciousness available to mankind. For over forty years, he labored to bring peace and enlightenment to our world. He taught that nothing is inevitable — not predicted earthquakes, nor the predicted negative side effects of the major astrological configurations, nor the destruction of the planet through our total disregard of her sacred nature and our rape of her resources.

One of Dr. King's outstanding early achievements was the global mission known as Operation Starlight. Way ahead of its time, this three-year mission, from 1958-1961, caused 19 mountains around the world to be charged with tremendous spiritual energy, making them New Age Power Centers. Dr. King had been instructed by highly elevated Masters to physically climb 18 of these 19 mountains, to be used as the "terrestrial anchor" for the charge that was to be put through him into these mountains.

Like giant batteries, these mountains now hold a charge that can be tapped by any good-thinking person who goes to these mountains and sends out prayers of healing for the world. The healing and power released by these pilgrims is equivalent to that which could be invoked by an Adept of energy manipulation. Operation Starlight therefore enables relatively ordinary people to bring about great change for the good on the surface of our world.

Pilgrimages

This leads to the final method of enhancing your Workout for the Soul that I will include in this book, which is making pilgrimages to the holy mountains for the reasons given above. If you really want to make a major difference to your own soul growth and to the world as a whole, and if you really want to experience tremendous spiritual power, then visit one of the mountains made holy in Operation Starlight. If you climb these places and conduct your prayers and healing on these sacred temples of nature, you will definitely notice the difference!

UNITED STATES OF AMERICA
    Mount Baldy (Southern California)
    Mount Tallac (Lake Tahoe, Northern California)
    Mount Adams (New Hampshire)
    Castle Peak (Aspen, Colorado)
GREAT BRITAIN
    Holdstone Down (Devonshire, England)
    Brown Willy (Cornwall, England)
    Ben Hope (The Highlands, Scotland)
    Craeg-An-Leth-Chain (Grampian, Scotland)
    Old Man of Coniston (Cumbria, England)
    Pen-Y-Fan (Powys, Wales)
    Carnedd Llywellyn (Gwynedd, Wales)
    Kinderscout (Derbyshire, England)
    Yes Tor (Devonshire, England)

AUSTRALIA
  Mount Kosciusko (New South Wales)
  Mount Ramshead (New South Wales)
NEW ZEALAND
  Mount Wakefield (South Island)
SWITZERLAND
  Madrigerfluh
FRANCE
  Le Nid d' Aigle (On the side of Mont Blanc)
TANZANIA (East Africa)
  Kilimanjaro

Further Information

For information on how to make pilgrimages to these Holy Mountains, as well as information about Dr. George King and activities of The Aetherius Society, please visit www.aetherius.org.

For further information about locations/activities in the U.S. and Canada, contact:
>
> The Aetherius Society
> 6202 Afton Place
> Hollywood, CA 90028
> Tel: (323) 465 9652
> Fax: (323) 462 5165
> Email: info@aetherius.org
>
> The Aetherius Society
> 17670 W. 12 Mile Road
> Southfield, MI 48076
> Tel: (248) 552-9153
> Fax: (248) 443-2337
> Email: aetheriusmi@cs.com

For further information about locations/activities in Europe, Africa, New Zealand or Australia, contact:

> The Aetherius Society
> 757 Fulham Road
> London, SW6 5UU
> England.
> Tel: (0207) 736 4187
> Fax: (0207) 731 1067
> Email: info@innerpotential.org
> Web site: www.innerpotential.org

For further details regarding this book, the author, seminars, lectures, classes, etc., please visit: www.chrissieblaze.com.

Bibliography

Abrahamson, Charles. *The Holy Mountains of the World.* Los Angeles: The Aetherius Society, 1994.

Bailey, Alice. *Esoteric Healing.* New York: Lucis Publishing Company, 1953.

Benson, Herbert. *The Relaxation Response.* New York: Avon Books, Inc., 1975.

Besant, Annie & C.W. Leadbeater. *Thought Forms.* Wheaton, IL: The Theosophical Publishing House, 1969.

Choa Kok Sui, *Pranic Healing.* York Beach, Maine: Samuel Weiser, 1990.

Dyer, Wayne W. *Manifest Your Destiny: The Nine Spiritual Principles for Getting Everything You Want.* New York: Harper Collins Publishers, 1999.

Hodson, Geoffrey. *Kingdom of the Gods.* Wheaton, IL: The Theosophical Publishing House, 1981.

Hunt, Roland. *The Seven Keys to Colour Healing.* Saffron Walden, England: C.W. Daniel, 1971.

King, George & Richard Lawrence. *Realize Your Inner Potential.* Los Angeles: The Aetherius Society, 1997.

King, George. *A Book of Sacred Prayers.* Los Angeles: The Aetherius Society, 1966.

King, George. *Concentration, Contemplation, Meditation.* Audio-cassette. Los Angeles: The Aetherius Society

King, George. *Cosmic Plan* audio-cassette. Los Angeles: The Aetherius Society.

King, George. *Contact Your Higher Self Through Yoga.* Los Angeles: The Aetherius Society, 1964.

King, George. *Karma and Reincarnation.* Los Angeles: The Aetherius Society, 1986.

King, George. *Imagination: Your Only Creative Faculty.* Audio-cassette. Los Angeles: The Aetherius Society.

King, George. *Man's Mind.* Audio-cassette. Los Angeles: The Aetherius Society.

King, George. *My Contact with the Great White Brotherhood.* Los Angeles: The Aetherius Society, 1965.

King, George. *Operation Sunbeam: God's Magic in Action.* Los Angeles: The Aetherius Society, 1979.

King, George. *Spiritual Healing.* Audio-tape of lecture. Los Angeles: The Aetherius Society, audiocassette.

King, George. *The Devic Kingdom.* Audio-tape of lecture. Los Angeles: The Aetherius Society.

King, George. *The Nine Freedoms.* Los Angeles: The Aetherius Society, 1974.

King, George. *The Truth About Dynamic Prayer.* London: The Aetherius Press, 1961.

King, George. *The Twelve Blessings.* London: The Aetherius Press, 1961.

King, George. *You Too Can Heal.* Los Angeles: The Aetherius Society, 1976.

Lawrence, Richard. *Journey into Supermind.* London, England: Souvenir Press, 1995.

Lawrence, Richard. *Unlock Your Pyschic Powers.* London, England: Souvenir Press, 1993.

Lawrence, Richard. *The Meditation Plan.* London, England: Judy Piatkus (Publishers) Ltd., 1999.

Norman Vincent Peale. *The Power of Positive Thinking.* New York: Ballantine Books, 1982.

Ouseley, S. G. *Colour Meditations.* Romford, Essex: L.N. Fowler, 1986.

Powell, A.E. *The Etheric Double.* London, England: The Theosophical Publishing House, 1987.

Ramacharaka, Yogi. *Advanced Course in Yogi Philosophy and Oriental Occultism.* Chicago: Yogi Publication Society, 1931.

Ramacharaka, Yogi. *Raja Yoga.* London: L.N. Fowler & Co. Ltd., 1979.

Ramacharaka, Yogi. *The Science of Breath .* London: L.N. Fowler & Co. Ltd., 1960.

Ryan, M.J. *Attitudes of Gratitude: How to Give and Receive Joy Every Day of Your Life.* Berkeley, CA: Conari Press, 1999.

Siegel, Bernie. *Love, Medicine & Miracles.* New York, Harper & Row, Publishers, Inc., 1990.

Shastri, Haris Prasad. *Meditation: Its Theory and Practice.* London: Shanti Sadan, 1958.

Sri Swami Sivananda. *Thought Power.* The Divine Life Society, Himalayas, India, 1996.

Swami Paramananda. *Faith is Power.* Vedanta Center, Cohasset, MA, 1985.

Thurston, Mark. *Soul-Purpose: Discovering and Fulfilling Your Destiny.* New York: St. Martin's Press, 1989.

Vivekananda. Swami. *Living at the Source.* Boston: Shambala Publications, 1993.

Vivekananda. Swami. *Karma Yoga.* Calcutta, India: Advaia Ashrama, 1974.

Vivekananda. Swami. *Raja-Yoga.* New York: Ramakrishna-Vivekananda Center, 1980.

Zi, Nancy. *The Art of Breathing.* Glendale, California: Vivi Company, 1997.

About the Author

Chrissie Blaze qualified as a teacher at the University of London, England. Her professional career ranges from teaching business studies in London colleges to working as the Director of a leading London investment company. She also certified as an astrologer at the Faculty of Astrological Studies, London, and practiced in this capacity in Europe and the U.S. Since 1996, she has lived in Los Angeles with her husband, Gary.

Chrissie regards her main career, however, as her lifelong study of the spiritual sciences. Her experience in this field includes teaching, writing, public relations, publicity and promotion, broadcasting and healing. Through regular radio and television broadcasts, lectures and workshops on subjects from spiritual development to UFO's, she has become a well-known figure in the New Age movement. Chrissie appeared regularly at the Festival for Mind-Body-Spirit, London, and has also appeared at the Whole Life Expo in Los Angeles.

In 1985, Chrissie was ordained in London by the Aetherius Church as one of the first female ministers in England. In 2000, she was appointed a Priest-Elect. In 1985, she became publicity officer for The Aetherius Society in Europe and helped launch several successful nationwide campaigns to raise awareness there. In 1994, Chrissie moved to the American headquarters of The Aetherius Society in Los Angeles to be closer to her Master, Dr. George King, until he passed away in 1997. Chrissie continues as publicity officer for The Aetherius Society in the U.S. This allows her to fulfill her goal of the global promotion of practical spirituality.

Titles Published by Aslan

The Candida Control Cookbook What You Should Know And What You Should Eat To Manage Yeast Infections
by Gail Burton
$14.95
ISBN 0-944031-67-6

Workout for the Soul: 8 Steps to Inner Fitness
by Chrissie Blaze
$14.95
ISBN 0-944031-90-0

The Gift of Wounding: Finding Hope & Heart in Challenging Circumstances
by Andre Auw Ph.D.
$13.95
ISBN 0-944031-79-X

How Loving Couples Fight: 12 Essential Tools for Working Through the Hurt
by James L Creighton Ph.D.
$16.95
ISBN 0-944031-71-4

Intuition Workout: A Practical Guide To Discovering & Developing Your Inner Knowing
by Nancy Rosanoff
$12.95
ISBN 0-944031-14-5

The Joyful Child: A Sourcebook of Activities and Ideas for Releasing Children's Natural Joy
by Peggy Jenkins Ph.D.
$16.95
ISBN 0-944031-66-8

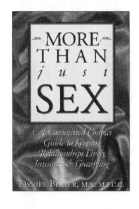

Lovers For Life: Creating
Lasting Passion, Trust
and True Partnership
by Daniel Ellenberg Ph.D.
& Judith Bell M.S., MFCC
$16.95
ISBN 0-944031-61-7

Magnificent Addiction:
Discovering Addiction as
Gateway to Healing
by Philip R. Kavanaugh, M.D.
$14.95
ISBN 0-944031-36-6

More Than Just Sex:
A Committed Couples
Guide to Keeping
Relationships Lively,
Intimate & Gratifying
by Daniel Beaver M.S., MFCC
$12.95
ISBN0-944031-35-8

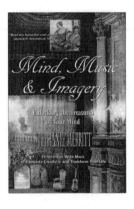

Mind, Music & Imagery:
Unlocking the Treasures
of Your Mind
by Stephanie Merritt
$13.95
ISBN 0-944031-62-5

New Woman Manager: 50
Fast & Savvy Solutions for
Executive Excellence
by Sharon Lamhut Willen
$14.95
ISBN 0-944031-11-0

The Motion Picture
Pre-scription Watch This
Movie and Call Me in The
Morning: 200 Movies to help
you heal life's problems
by Gary Solomon Ph.D.
"The Movie Doctor "
$12.95
ISBN 0-944031-27-7

Solstice Evergreen: The History, Folklore & Origins of the Christmas Tree 2nd ed by Sheryl Karas
$14.95
ISBN 0-944031-75-7

What Happened to the Prince I Married: Spiritual Healing for a Wounded Relationship by Sirah Vettese Ph.D.
$14.95
ISBN 0-944031-76-5

If You Want to be Rich & Happy Don't Go to School: Ensuring Lifetime Security for Yourself & Your Children by Robert T. Kiyosaki
$15.95
ISBN 0-944031-59-5

More Aslan Titles

Facing Death, Finding Love: The Healing Power Of Grief & Loss in One Family's Life by Dawson Church, $10.95; ISBN 0-944031-31-5

Gentle Roads to Survival: Making Self-Healing Choices in Difficult Circumstances by Andre Auw Ph.D. $10.95; ISBN 0-944031-18-8

Lynn Andrews in Conversation with Michael Toms edited by Hal Zina Bennett, $8.95; ISBN 0-944031-42-0

Argument With An Angel by Jan Cooper, $11.95; ISBN 0-944031-63-3

To order any of Aslan's titles send a check or money order for the price of the book plus Shipping & Handling

Book Rate $3 for 1st book.; $1.00 for each additional book
First Class $4 for 1st book; $1.50 for each additional book

Send to: ***Aslan Publishing***
2490 Black Rock Turnpike # 342
Fairfield CT 06432

To receive a current catalog: please call (800) 786–5427 or (203) 372–0300
E-mail us at: **info@aslanpublishing.com**
Visit our website at **www.aslanpublishing.com**

Our authors are available for seminars, workshops, and lectures. For further information or to reach a specific author, please call or email Aslan Publishing.

Revised & Expanded

Your Body Believes Every Word You Say

The Language of the Body/Mind Connection

With a section on Dreams & Drawings by
Bernie S. Siegel, M.D.

Barbara Hoberman Levine

"My twenty years of medical practice has confirmed the truth found in Your Body Believes Every Word You Say. Barbara's message is an eye-opener."

Christiane Northrup M. D.,
Author of Women's Bodies, Women's Wisdom.

Levine's book:

- shows how to avoid dis-easing language that sabotages your wellness

- lists hundreds of common expres sions we use unconsciously every day and illustrates how these seedthoughts can set us up for illness

- teaches how to decode physical sensations in order to discover the underlying seedthoughts and core beliefs

- describes how to draw up a customized Operating Manual that you can use to keep your body healthy

- contains detailed instructions for over 50 self-help experiences

- teaches powerful holistic healing techniques

- shows how to bring disease-causing ideas from your subconscious to your conscious mind-and reprogram your life dramatically for the better

"In simple, non-medical terminology, Levine's inspiring story demonstrates how, instead of remaining a passive victim, you can use illness as a tool for increased self-understanding and, ultimately, healing."
Rabbi Steven Rosman author of Jewish Healing Wisdom

"Barbara Levine's journey is one of courage and growth. We can all learn from her experience. She shows us what we are capable of and how to achieve our full healing potential."
Bernie Siegel, M. D., Author of Love, Medicine, and Miracles

0-88331-219-0 (trade paper) $16.95

WordsWorkPress.com